The Lawyer's Guide to Negotiation

Second Edition

X.M. FRASCOGNA, JR. AND H. LEE HETHERINGTON

AMERICAN BAR ASSOCIATION
General Practice, Solo & Small Firm Division

Cover design by ABA Publishing.

Printed in the United States of America.
13 12 11 10 09 5 4 3 2 1

Cataloging-in-Publication Data is on file with the Library of Congress

The Lawyer's Guide to Negotiation, Second Edition / X.M. Frascogna, Jr. and H. Lee Hetherington
ISBN: 978-1-60442-578-9

2008022202

Discounts are available for books ordered in bulk. Special consideration is given to state bars, CLE programs, and other bar-related organizations. Inquire at Book Publishing, ABA Publishing, American Bar Association, 321 North Clark Street, Chicago, Illinois 60654-7598

www.ababooks.org

Contents

Acknowledgments

We first want to thank those individuals at the American Bar Association who have contributed to making this third edition of *The Lawyer's Guide to Negotiation: A Strategic Approach to Better Contracts and Settlement's* a reality. They include Rick Paszkiet, and all the lawyers in the ABA's General Practice, Solo and Small Firm Section who so generously volunteered their time to read and comment on the manuscript.

This book could not have been written without the many contributions of our colleagues, friends, and students, who, over the years, have consciously and unconsciously provided us with ideas, theories, and fresh approaches to the fascinating topic of negotiation.

We would especially like to thank, in alphabetical order, Dr. Tony Alessandra, Paul Benton, Peggy Brown, Janice Carden, Rick Courtney, Ryanne Duffie, Terry Duffie, Wayne Ferrell, Pat Frascogna, Jim Kitchens, Henry Green, Kristie Hairston, Matt Hetzel, Shawnassey Britt, Ron Jurney, Danny Keen, Professor Randy Lowery, Hunter Lundy, David Maddox, Mike Maloney, Brenda Marsalis, Joe Moak, Jack Mohler, Michelle Partridge, Jim Powell, Ouida Rainey, Dan Robinson, Tom Stingley, Bob Tyler, Earl Walker, Professor Carol C. West, Doug Williams, Melvin Williams, Tommy Wolf, and all of our colleagues on the law faculty of Mississippi College School of Law.

Finally, thanks goes to all of our negotiation students from over the years at Mississippi College School of Law, Catholic University of America School of Law, Loyola Law School of Los Angeles, and Whittier Law School. While this book was written primarily for your benefit, we have been the ultimate beneficiaries.

1

Law Practice Is Negotiation

§ 1.01 Introduction

Law practice is negotiation. Whether you are attempting to conclude an acquisition agreement, trying to settle a personal injury claim, or conferring with a client about pending legal matters, you are negotiating. In the final analysis, all of a lawyer's legal training and professional expertise is directed toward one objective—solving the client's problems. Negotiation is the primary tool for doing just that. Consequently, lawyers who cannot effectively negotiate cannot effectively practice law.

While every lawyer will undoubtedly agree that negotiation is an important skill, few view it as the single most important factor to the overall success of their practice. Be assured that it is. Negotiation is by far the most frequently used device to resolve conflicts and claims. Negotiation is the only process available to form and give order to business relationships. It is the process that combines legal training and experience with interpersonal skills to achieve tangible results. We like to think of negotiation as being the action side of a law practice.

To illustrate this point, consider the following:

- More than 95 percent of all civil claims are concluded by negotiation, not litigation.
- Of those claims that actually go to trial, only a fraction go to verdict, and of those that do, a substantial portion are settled by negotiation pending appeal.
- Every conceivable type of business relationship is created by negotiation.
- The overwhelming majority of inmates currently serving time in United States penal institutions are there because of a negotiated plea bargain.

§ 1.02 Making the Most of Your Natural Advantage as a Lawyer

Lawyers enjoy a decided advantage when it comes to negotiation. While the reasons for this are both real and imagined, the fact remains that lawyers have a head start over the layperson in the give and take of negotiation.

A primary reason for this advantage is public perception. The average layperson views lawyers as being naturally superior negotiators. This is true even in matters having little or nothing to do with legal issues. After all, giant corporations such as Microsoft, Viacom, and Toyota turn to legal counsel when putting together multimillion-dollar deals. Professional quarterbacks, rock stars, and network television personalities usually rely on their lawyers rather than themselves when negotiating big-money contracts. Even the United States government finds it necessary to retain high-powered Wall Street lawyers to help diplomats deal with complex foreign-policy trade negotiations such as the North American Free Trade Agreement, General Agreement on Tariffs and Trade, and Trade-Related Aspects of Intellectual Property Rights. It just stands to reason that lawyers "must" be superior negotiators.

In reality, this perception of superiority based on the mere fact of law school graduation and bar passage is not always accurate. Lawyers have no more of an inherent claim on proficient negotiation skills than anyone else. The plain fact is that negotiation is a learned skill. It was not until the 1990s that American law schools finally began to emphasize negotiation and other essential lawyering skills within the context of their curricula.

Prompted by the findings and recommendations of the MacCrate Commission, law schools began to elevate practical skills such as negotiation, interviewing, and client counseling to a level previously enjoyed by traditional substantive offerings such as contracts, torts, property, and civil procedure. The popular view in legal education prior to the skills movement was that negotiation was something lawyers could pick up in practice. And, while that view makes very little sense today, many members of the bar had no alternative but to learn from trial and error.

Given the new emphasis on bargaining skills and problem solving, together with the fact that lawyers are simply exposed to more negotiation situations than nonlawyers, the public perception that members of the bar are superior negotiators is, for the most part, well-founded. But that does not mean that there is not room for improvement.

§ 1.03 The New Paradigm of Law Practice: Problem Solving

Most lawyers are generally adequate negotiators and will win their share of negotiations. But experience teaches that lawyers are not satisfied with just being adequate or merely winning their share.

Combine this basic truism with the new realities of practicing law in the digital age, and it becomes readily apparent that developing negotiation proficiency can no longer be left to chance. This is illustrated by the monumental changes brought about by the emergence of the so-called "new economics." Within the past five to ten years, as the world economy has changed in response to the information and communications revolution, the legal profession has become much more diversified and grown increasingly complex. The new model for the modern lawyer is that of a cooperative problem solver working in a team environment. The modern lawyer is retained today as much for his ability to overcome problems, break through stalemates, and provide an overall framework for economic growth as for his knowledge of fine points of law. The line between legal advice and business advice has blurred. The lawyer is increasingly viewed as an indispensable player in the modern economy who not only helps clients navigate the legal system, but also plays a key role in making things happen through an understanding of people, their work environments, and problems and challenges.

This new paradigm makes the ability to build bridges through effective negotiation more important than it has ever been within the context of a legal practice. This book is written specifically for lawyers making that adjustment. It seeks to dispel some long-held myths while offering lawyers a consistent approach that will provide the necessary framework for any bargaining challenge within the context of an evolving style of practicing law on a much broader landscape.

§ 1.04 Universal Principles and Concepts of Negotiation

The first discovery all young lawyers have to make is that negotiation is not as mysterious or elusive as most would have them believe. The lawyers who negotiate multimillion-dollar, international business agreements do not do it with mirrors or sleight of hand. Rather, they employ basic, time-tested principles and concepts of leverage, timing, knowledge, preparation, and determination to achieve the end result. Instead of searching for magic solutions, these lawyers simply rely on the recurrent patterns and principles of negotiation that have existed ever since two prehistoric cavemen exchanged fire to be used for light and warmth as a quid pro quo for a smooth, heavy rock that could be used for protection.

These basic principles are still at work today in law and business offices and courtrooms around the world without regard to the disarming simplicity of the issue or the cutting edge complexity of the problem or the dollar amount involved.

§ 1.05 The Negotiating Lesson from Iran

One of the most dramatic negotiations the world has ever witnessed involved the release of the 53 American hostages from captivity in Iran. On January 20, 1981, after 444 days, the hostages were finally released by virtue of a negotiated settlement directed by President Carter's White House. It is no coincidence that the American captives were being sped to the Tehran Airport at the precise moment the presidential oath was being administered to Ronald Reagan, half a world away.

Why? The Iranians were greatly influenced by the power of deadlines. They knew that once the transfer of power to the Reagan administration was completed, the negotiating environment would change radically. The new administration promised to take a harder line with Iran. The result: an agreement after 15 months of deadlock. This deadline factor combined with the uncertainty of a new administration—plus the fact that Iran had already gained maximum publicity value from the hostages and desperately needed money to conduct its war with Iraq—resulted in the agreement that delivered the hostages' freedom.

This well-known example stresses the point that there are, indeed, negotiation principles and concepts that can begin working for you immediately. The key is learning to recognize these concepts and understanding how and why they work. The modern negotiator knows that a calculated and planned approach to bargaining based on these principles will always prevail over reliance on a bag of random tricks. Understanding these controlling concepts will allow you to address any problem that circumstances may dictate, to remain unruffled when the tactic that has always worked before fails, or when the other side remains indifferent after you play what you thought was your trump card. This is the difference between an adequate negotiator and an accomplished negotiator in a modern practice setting.

§ 1.06 There Are No Rules

While there are basic principles, concepts, strategies, tactics, and techniques that give form to the negotiation process, there are no rules by which the game is played—except the rules you make, or the ones you allow your bargaining counterpart to make.

To illustrate, consider the following: A resident of Illinois comes to you claiming he has sustained damages in the amount of $100,000 resulting from the alleged negligence of the defendant, a resident of California. Based on this claim, you advise the plaintiff to file suit in federal district court based on diversity of citizenship. As plaintiff's attorney, you can rely on the Federal Rules of Civil Procedure to provide a framework for the procedural development of your action. Likewise, you know that the rules of evidence will govern admissibility of proof at trial. All of these rules are uniform and binding on both parties. They provide some assurance that the defendant will file a timely responsive pleading and that each side will have an adequate opportunity to seek relevant facts through discovery. They also help minimize surprise, delay, or admission of prejudiced statements based on hearsay or undue influence. The primary drawbacks to using the judicial system to resolve this conflict are the expense and length of time involved. This point takes on added significance where the parties have weaknesses or proof problems with their case, or where the amount of money involved would make it uneconomical to proceed to trial.

An alternative to litigation for both parties is to seek a negotiated settlement that could be quicker and less expensive. Assuming this course of action is adopted, the parties, especially the plaintiff, will quickly begin to realize there are no uniform rules of negotiation to ensure fairness, guard against delay, and otherwise guide the negotiation in a predictable, logical manner. The only rules are the ones the parties elect to adopt.

For example, if you, as the plaintiff's lawyer, write a demand letter to the defendant, there is nothing that requires the defendant to comply with your demand. In fact, the defendant need not respond to the letter. If he does choose to respond, there is no time limit within which he must do so. Assuming the defendant does elect to respond, he controls both the substance and form of that response.

The point to remember is that you as a negotiator are in a position to create, accept, and reject the rules by which a given negotiation will be conducted. Lawyers who recognize and make the most of this fundamental negotiation principle will enjoy a decided advantage over those who allow their opponents to make the rules.

§ 1.07 Constraints That Limit a Negotiator's Freedom of Action

While there are no rules governing a negotiation, there are certain constraints that limit a negotiator's freedom of action. Some apply across the board to all negotiators, while others are only applicable to lawyers.

§ 1.08 Illegal Conduct

Lawyers and nonlawyers alike are limited by sanctions against illegal conduct, such as fraud, coercion, and conspiracy. While these provisions by no means ensure honesty and fair dealing, they do set a minimal standard of conduct below which most negotiators are unwilling to venture.

§ 1.09 Ethics Codes

In addition to legal sanctions, the American Bar Association's Model Rules of Professional Conduct, along with any specific state and local rules bearing on attorney ethics, provide a check on a lawyer's conduct in a negotiation.

§ 1.10 Professional Reputation

A practical constraint on a lawyer's negotiating style is her own professional reputation. While a lawyer is entitled and even required to pursue a client's interests zealously within the bounds of legal and ethics codes, lawyers must take care not to sacrifice their reputations and credibility by engaging in conduct detrimental not only to the client but to the lawyer as well. Winning at all costs may have the effect of reducing or destroying a lawyer's long-term credibility. Representation of a client's interests must be balanced by a sense of propriety and reputation with the practicing bar.

§ 1.11 Effectiveness

A lawyer's approach to a negotiation will also be constrained by her ability to achieve workable solutions to a client's long-term as well as short-term problems. For example, assume a lawyer is in a position to negotiate a totally one-sided contract in a client's favor by virtue of superior leverage and the lawyer's understanding of the negotiation process. The client will obviously be pleased in the short run. However, if the contract proves to be so burdensome to the other side as to be unworkable, the other party may find breach preferable to performance. Should this be the case, the client who was initially satisfied with the negotiated contract will be deprived of his primary objective—a workable agreement.

Clients are seldom pleased to find out that they have to litigate what they thought they had already secured through negotiation. Even if the client should win in court, he is still a loser in terms of lost time and expense. The lesson is to negotiate the most advantageous contract possible for your client that the other side can accept with. To go any further becomes potentially self-defeating.

§ 1.12 Constraints Are Rarely Uniform

In addition to recognizing the constraints to a negotiation, lawyers should be aware that these constraints will rarely be applied uniformly. For example, while all lawyers are bound by applicable ethics codes, there is a wide divergence of acceptable ethical conduct within the Model Rules.

Technically, opposing lawyers may be in compliance, while the realities and consequences of their behavior are in marked contrast. It is crucial to understand these types of disparities so as not to fall victim to an adversary who may be playing the same game by a different set of rules. Probably the worst miscalculation one can make is to assume that everyone sees the world from your perspective, ethically and otherwise. To borrow President Ronald Reagan's memorable quote to then Soviet General Secretary Mikhail Gorbachev at the 1986 summit in Reykjavik, Iceland, "Trust but verify."

§ 1.13 The Client Understands Only the Bottom Line

All lawyers know that the client is the ultimate judge of their efforts. The client may not understand or fully appreciate the intricacies of the law or your ability to grasp and deal with complex legal problems. The client does, however, understand one thing—results! The negotiation process is the primary vehicle to achieving bottom- line results.

The purpose of this book is to help you improve your negotiation skills to the point where you win more than just "your share." An understanding of the recurring patterns and principles of negotiation, coupled with an awareness of how and when to use this knowledge, will pay immediate dividends to you and your clients in terms of bottom-line results. Ultimately, that is what practicing law is really all about.

§ 1.14 Looking Back to See Forward

Most lawyers are destined to have an abundance of negotiating experiences during their careers. Whether you are a young lawyer just beginning your legal practice, the experienced veteran of 40 years, or the many lawyers whose careers fall somewhere in between, you all have one thing in common—the need to negotiate effectively. Because negotiation is such a frequently used skill, lawyers tend to become fairly proficient at it. Whether it's litigation, mediation, cooperation, or simply communication, all of these forms of persuasion can be used as part of the negotiating process. Since negotiation has been practiced from the very beginning of human interaction, it is often valuable to look to the past to catch a glimpse of how to skillfully use the negotiation process in the future.

§ 1.15 The Great War and Rubius Gallos

During the Great War of the Jews against the Romans in 70 A.D., the last resistance of the Jews was the rock fortress of Masada in the Judaean desert. This formidable and seemingly impregnable structure sat on a mountaintop some 1,424 feet above the Dead Sea. The rock of this ancient mountain fortress rose 820 feet on the east side and over 600 feet on the west.

Originally, this superstructure had been built in 36 B.C. as a safe haven for Herod the Great and his family. After Herod's death, a Roman garrison held the fortress until the Jewish Revolt. Eventually, the Jews overran the Roman garrison and held Masasda throughout the Great War. As Rome began the process of recapturing its lost territory, Masada was the last stronghold to stand after Jerusalem fell to the Romans.

Growing impatient and beginning to feel political pressure from the Senate, Emperor Vespasian ordered the Tenth Legion under the command of Flavius Silva to crush the Jewish resistance at Masada. With 5,000 soldiers and over 9,000 slaves and prisoners of war, Silva stationed his troops along the slopes of Masada and lay siege to the fortress. The Romans constructed a ramp of packed earth and stones and erected a siege tower. Under cover of fire from its top, they moved the tower with its battering ram up the ramp.

Once the siege tower was in place, the Romans began pounding the wall of the fortress. Eventually, it became obvious the mighty wall would crumble and the Romans would overrun the 900 occupants of Masada. On the eve of the day it appeared inevitable to both sides that Masada would fall to the Romans, the Jews made a decision that would deny the Romans a total victory. The next day, as the wall was finally breached and Roman soldiers stormed into the city, they found that all the occupants of Masada had taken their lives.

The mastermind of the plan to retake Masada was an old Roman siege master, Rubius Gallos. Silva had personally recalled Gallos from Rome to develop and implement a plan to capture Masada. During one of Gallos's many inspections of the ramp prior to the final assault, he was gravely wounded by a Jewish archer. Although Gallos was immediately rushed to the surgeons, they were unable to save him. As he lay on his deathbed, he gave Silva and his staff his final instructions on how to complete the attack. He detailed the angle that the battering ram should be positioned, the time of day of the attack, and the particular units to lead the assault. Just as Gallos was completing his instructions, he died. However, he was able to relay enough information to Silva and his staff for them to complete construction of the ramp and siege tower and execute his assault plan.

The predicament of Rubius Gallos brings into focus a fundamental question: What is really important in a negotiation? What must you know and apply every time you negotiate? Stated differently, if you were in Rubius Gallos's situation, what essential negotiation wisdom would you pass on to those intently listening to your every word? Assuming time was quickly slipping away, could you do it in 20 seconds or less?

§ 1.16 Everything You Need to Know About Negotiation in 20 Seconds

Everything you need to know to conduct a successful negotiation is contained in the answers to four questions:

- With whom am I dealing?
- What do I want?
- How will I go about getting what I want?
- What are the unique circumstances?

The answers to these four questions will obviously vary from one negotiation to the next. However, the answers always lead to the information needed to be successful at the bargaining table. The answer to the question "With whom am I dealing?" identifies the personality type of the individual across the table, which in turn reveals negotiating style and patterns, always helpful information in any negotiation.

Every astute negotiator knows the answer to the question "What do I want?" before entering the negotiation arena. How a negotiation unfolds strategically has to do with the answer to the "How will I go about getting what I want?" question. And every prepared negotiator looks at the specific circumstances in which the negotiation is taking place.

The first step in any negotiation plan should always begin by posing the four Rubius Gallos questions. Clearly define your responses to these crucial questions before time runs out.

PRACTICE TIP: There are no rules to the negotiation game except the rules you make or the ones you allow your opponent to make.

2
The Power of Leverage

§ 2.01 Introduction

Plaintiffs' lawyers are acutely aware that insurance companies do not settle personal injury claims just to help judges clear crowded dockets or to enable unfortunate accident victims to improve their lots in life. These companies are motivated by one thing—their own self-interest. By paying $50,000 to settle a case, an insurer avoids the uncertainty of an adverse jury verdict that might require it to pay significantly more than the settlement amount.

Self-interest is also the principle that controls the creation of all business relations. Obviously, television networks do not pay huge sums for the rights to broadcast college and professional football games just to give their commentators and cameramen something to do on Saturday and Sunday afternoons. They are motivated by the leverage of financial opportunity. The networks fully expect to see a return in excess of their investment, just as all businesses and investors do. In terms of a negotiated change in the status quo, self-interest is expressed as leverage. In effect, parties to a negotiated agreement gain and make concessions to achieve their goals by means of specific actions based on the universal concepts of leverage.

These fundamental concepts of leverage, manifested in various forms, are what experienced bargainers have always used to foster change in the status quo. The good news is that the principles of leverage have been in existence from the very first barter transaction that surely took place long before recorded history. Principles of leverage can be classified into one of four easy-to-understand and use categories. In most negotiations, two or more of these principles will be at work. Often, all four can be found. The trick is to adapt them to the particular facts, circumstances, and objectives of the negotiation at hand.

§ 2.02 Leverage Derives Its Power from Self-Interest

The power of leverage is grounded on the most basic premise of human existence—self-interest. Except in instances of pure altruism, people are moved to action only when their self-interest is served. Whether self-interest is defined as avoiding potential liability, obtaining financial gain, or any number of less tangible objectives such as the attainment of good will, improved labor relations, or a heightened degree of prestige, the governing principle remains the same. Consequently, it is vital that negotiators fully understand their self-interest in terms of specific goals and objectives. It is equally if not more important to understand your negotiating counterpart's self-interest. Chapter 4 on preparation provides a systematic approach to this all-important task.

A second characteristic of leverage is its ability to change and adapt to the unfolding drama and quickly developing circumstances against which any given negotiation is conducted. Because leverage is by no means a static concept, a lawyer's success in exerting influence will naturally depend on the specific objective sought, the personalities of the people involved, and the circumstances that exist at any particular point in the negotiation. For example, if you represent a highly paid young wage earner who has been permanently disabled after being struck by a speeding automobile driven by an intoxicated millionaire in plain view of a dozen witnesses, it would be safe to say that you would enjoy a rather strong leverage position. Unfortunately for lawyers, cases involving clear liability or nonliability do not come along every day. More commonly, each side will have strengths and weaknesses. The winner is often determined by who is more resourceful and astute in identifying, assessing, and using the power of leverage.

Regardless of whether you are handling a typical small claims matter or a complex, high-stakes negotiation, the key to extracting concessions and realizing your objectives is leverage.

To illustrate, consider some of the events that have occurred during recent presidential administrations. President George H.W. Bush, confronted with the bully tactics of Saddam Hussein, found himself engaged in a high-stakes game of "chicken." Saddam issued the challenge, and President Bush reacted, based on his leverage position. The result—Operation Desert Storm.

Thirteen years later, President Bush's son, George W. Bush, found his administration engaged with his father's nemesis in another high-stakes negotiation. This struggle for international power, however, resulted in Saddam's ultimate defeat and death.

The impeachment of President Clinton afforded a remarkable view of leverage at work. Both President Clinton and his opponents used political leverage throughout the impeachment proceeding to shift national opinion. At times, it appeared President Clinton's political adversaries would force him to vacate the Oval Office. Then leverage exerted by President Clinton's supporters would shift public opinion in favor of the president. In the end, President Clinton's leverage prevailed.

Another classic example of leverage at work unfolded during President Reagan's administration when he was confronted by the Professional Air Traffic Controllers Organization (PATCO) strike.

§ 2.03 The PATCO Strike: Leverage on a National Scale

In August 1981, President Reagan was confronted with his first major domestic crisis—the air controllers' strike. The controllers sought more money for fewer hours of work in the name of fairness and in the interest of public safety. In the beginning, it appeared that the air controllers union had the upper hand in the confrontation with the government. The threat of thousands of air controllers leaving their jobs across the country was indeed a powerful negotiating lever.

The economic concerns of the airline industry and the public's safety fears, not to mention America's commercial and personal dependence on air transport, made PATCO's bargaining position very appealing. In fact, PATCO's position appeared to be invincible. Surely the administration would have to do something to placate the controllers with so much at stake. However, in the end, the air controllers either returned to work without any wage increase or were fired. What happened to cause such a reversal of leverage strength resulting in the total failure of the union's demands?

Why PATCO lost its leverage: Despite a strong leverage position, PATCO's leadership miscalculated the strength of its leverage in several ways. The first was an error of perception. The union negotiators on this issue failed to understand the personality of President Reagan. The president had adopted a position supported by personal conviction that, no matter how deserving they might be, PATCO's members were threatening to violate a no-strike provision in their contract with the government. Not only was this tactic illegal, it was a direct assault on one of the president's personal principles, thus requiring him to assume an uncompromising stance. The union simply did not weigh the personality of one of the key players in the drama.

The second major problem revolved around precedent. President Reagan reasoned that if he compromised with PATCO, the die would be cast and a clear message sent to more than two million federal employees who were also suffering from the ravages of inflation. The potential loss for the administration became much greater than simply a few concessions with a small union. Any concession would be a message to federal employees who had one eye on their paychecks and the other on the evening news. PATCO's threats to the administration's self-interest suddenly took on monumental proportions.

> Another explanation for PATCO's loss of leverage was their evaluation of the circumstances surrounding the negotiations with the government. While many Americans were sympathetic to the air controllers' pleas, the prevailing mood of the country at the time was negative toward wage increases for any particular segment, especially government. This mood had been brought about by the nation's fear of then-escalating inflation coupled with recession and alarm over growing federal budget deficits.
>
> The final straw that broke the union's back was its use of its leverage position. In the beginning, PATCO evoked sympathy and concern from Americans by demonstrating that its demands were both legitimate and reasonable. However, as the strike deadline neared, the union's position hardened. It became all or nothing.
>
> Suddenly, public sentiment began to shift to the president. The controllers were perceived as being greedy, unreasonable, and totally unwilling to seek an equitable solution. This was borne out by the fact that the union had overwhelmingly rejected an apparent settlement that would have brought them some relief while also averting a strike. Talks broke off. Instead of attempting to find a way to make progress on their demands and to allow the administration a way to save face, the union resorted to tough talk and more threats.
>
> In response, the president made a threat of his own that had the support of the American people; either return to the control towers or lose your job. Quite simply, the president was prepared to risk the consequences of having to replace the controllers. As soon as this decision was made, the controllers lost their primary leverage position. As we all know, PATCO carried out its threat, and the president carried out his. The loser: PATCO.

The air controllers' strike is a prime example of the limits of leverage and the importance of knowing what to do with it once you've got it.

PRACTICE TIP: Leverage is the power, or ability, to motivate or persuade others to adopt your position, or a position more favorable to your position.

---

§ 2.04 How to Calculate Your Leverage Position

The first step to successfully influencing the actions of others through leverage is to make a realistic assessment of the circumstances surrounding your client's problem. Every negotiation can be classified in one of three categories based on an analysis of your alternatives to a negotiated agreement. Naturally, the more alternatives you have, the more leverage you can exert against your opponent. This assessment will play a major role in the tactics and strategies you select during a negotiation.

The three basic categories are:

1. The Lost Opportunity Alternative
2. The "Or Else" Alternative
3. The Litigated Alternative

§ 2.05 The Lost Opportunity Alternative

The alternative to agreement in most business negotiations falls into the "lost opportunity" category. Lost opportunity is characterized by parties seeking to achieve mutual benefits by means of a negotiated agreement. A common example is a transaction involving the purchase and sale of real estate. Both the seller and buyer stand to benefit from reaching an agreement, provided the terms can be worked out to the mutual satisfaction of the parties. However, if an agreement is not reached, the parties have lost nothing more than the time they have invested in the negotiation and a potential opportunity. The importance the parties place on the specific lost opportunity will directly determine its relative leverage value. The greater the potential loss of opportunity, the greater the advantage to the other party.

The typical lost opportunity negotiation is generally characterized by alternatives on both sides. In an ordinary real estate transaction, there will be other potential buyers and sellers. This even split of alternatives begins to shift as the circumstances move away from the norm. For example, suppose the real estate in question happens to be a residence located on Monterey Peninsula's famed Seventeen Mile Drive bordering Pebble Beach Golf Course in California. Further assume that the buyer is a wealthy golfer whose lifetime dream has been to own a home at Pebble Beach.

For the buyer, money is certainly a factor, but it is not the overriding consideration. Obviously, if the seller's lawyer has access to this information, his leverage position would be greatly strengthened, thereby allowing him to seek a higher selling price and more favorable terms. Alternatively, the buyer's attorney would attempt to project a posture of only passing interest so as not to provide the seller with increased leverage while attempting to make the most of his own position.

§ 2.06 The "Or Else" Alternative

This type of negotiation involves a situation in which the solution to the problem could benefit all parties. The alternative to a negotiated solution is an undesirable result in which all parties stand to lose. The classic example of the "or else" alternative is collective bargaining between labor and management. A negotiated agreement yields certainty and assures smooth operation for management while providing stable compensation and fringe benefits for labor. The alternative is a strike in which both labor and management would suffer. Where the parties simply cannot or will not reach agreement, the ultimate leverage advantage will focus on which party is in a better position to out-suffer the other.

The baseball strike: Major league baseball has experienced several labor disruptions in the past, the most serious of which led to cancellation of the 1994 World Series. However, the first player strike in 1981 is most illustrative of the "or else" alternative in terms of the link between alternatives and leverage. After months of talks, the players and owners were at a stalemate over the issue of compensation to be paid by teams signing free agents. The players' primary leverage was the threat of a strike that would shut down the ballparks and deprive the owners of gate receipts and television and radio revenue—a seemingly powerful lever.

On the downside, the players were risking their salaries, which were considerable by normal standards. The players reasoned that a strike would hurt the owners more than themselves, thus providing leverage for an ultimate concession on the compensation issue. Their assessment was probably correct, except for one additional factor. The owners had anticipated the players' leverage and responded by purchasing strike insurance. The policy provided each owner with a payment of $50,000 for each game not played if the players did strike, which at the time was worth considerably more in real dollars. Additionally, the owners would not have to meet player payrolls except in the few cases where some superstars had contract clauses requiring a continuation of their salaries in the event of a strike.

As the summer wore on, the owners were in no hurry to hammer out an agreement with the players. Two days after the strike insurance expired, a settlement was reached. The relative leverage positions had changed. The owners were no longer in a position to accept more pain than was being inflicted on the players. The result was a new agreement.

§ 2.07 The Litigated Alternative

Negotiations involving claims that, if not settled by negotiation, would be determined by a judge or jury fall under the heading of the litigated alternative. Usually, in these situations, the gain of one party is tied to the loss of another.

The most common illustration of the "litigated alternative" is the personal injury claim. The plaintiff seeks a financial settlement with the defendant's insurance company based on alleged legal liability of the defendant. The alternative to a negotiated settlement is to seek a monetary judgment that will be potentially higher than the negotiated conclusion. The best the defendant can hope for is a judgement of no liability. Even in total victory, the defendant will usually have to absorb attorney fees.

In this situation, the law supplies the plaintiff with leverage by compelling the defendant to either settle the claim or be exposed to legal liability, provided the plaintiff is able to state a cause of action and sustain the burden of proof. The defendant's leverage revolves around weaknesses in the plaintiff's case. The settlement value will depend on the relevant facts and law, as well as the plaintiff's ability to create uncertainty in the mind of the defendant.

A plaintiff with a marginal claim supported by weak evidence poses no great danger to a well-financed insurance company beyond the nuisance value of the suit. As any defense lawyer will verify, there is a world of difference between filing a lawsuit and winning one.

The litigated alternative clearly favors lawyers over the rest of the world. As one lawyer succinctly put it to a nonlawyer in the midst of a heated dispute, "Lawsuits are free for me." The seemingly intractable dispute was quickly resolved. This reality helps explain why lawyers enjoy a natural advantage in bargaining, especially in a dispute resolution context. It also gives substance to the perception widely held by nonlawyers that the legal profession should not be taken lightly at the bargaining table. If you appreciate this advantage, you can profit from this perception.

§ 2.08 The Four Levers You Can Use to Maximize Your Bargaining Position

No two negotiations are ever identical. The circumstances, personalities, and bargaining strength of each party will vary with each new situation. Consequently, the specific means employed to influence your opponent's actions will differ depending on these variables. There are, however, four fundamental, time-tested levers you can employ in every situation to help maximize your bargaining position. They are:

1. Uncertainty
2. Time
3. Opportunity
4. Sanction

The skilled negotiator is like the military commander perched atop a hill overlooking the battlefield. As he observes the deployment and movement of troops, he responds with the appropriate force—air power, sea power, or ground troops. The negotiator has at his disposal the levers of uncertainty, sanction, opportunity, or time. Every tactic used in a negotiation can be traced back to one of these forms of leverage.

PRACTICE TIP: One or more of these levers will always provide bargaining power no matter how complex or unique the situation. When used appropriately, they can increase your prospects for a successful outcome in any negotiation situation.

---

§ 2.09 Uncertainty

Because uncertainty is one of man's greatest natural enemies, it is the most powerful of the four levers. Uncertainty uses the element of the unknown to influence the actions and decisions of others.

People tend to worry far more about an anticipated event than the reality of that event once it has taken place. It is this basic fear of the unknown that motivates people to seek as much certainty as possible in their lives. The certain and safe present is always preferred to the uncertain and potentially dangerous future. This is precisely why the lever of uncertainty is such an effective tool in influencing the actions of others. It rests on the premise that people fear taking action. It follows that people are willing to pay handsomely to trade uncertainty for certainty. The person who can tolerate the highest level of uncertainty will enhance his negotiation leverage.

Uncertainty is built into the legal system: Uncertainty applies to all negotiations, particularly for the legal profession. This stems from the fact that uncertainty is central to the entire judicial system. The courts represent the last resort to failed negotiations. If you are attempting to negotiate differences, there is at least some element of certainty and control left to the negotiating participants. However, once the matter is referred to a judge or jury, the dispute enters the realm of uncertainty.

While the lawyer is still involved in the litigation process, the ultimate decision-making authority has shifted from lawyer and client to judge and jury. Once the dispute reaches trial, lawyers can only try to predict the outcome. While the lawyer's prediction is certainly an educated one, based on an evaluation of the law, facts, and overall presentation, it is still speculation. The results: anxiety brought on by uncertainty.

Due to the pressures of uncertainty, defendants are moved to settle cases for more than they feel the claim is reasonably worth when faced with maximum exposure that can be 10, 20, or even 30 times the settlement amount. Alternatively, plaintiffs must weigh the uncertainty of a fixed-sum settlement offer that is substantially below the possible verdict amount. It is precisely this factor of uncertainty that motivates plaintiffs and defendants to settle more than 95 percent of all disputed legal claims.

Uncertainty applies to every negotiation situation: While the litigated alternative situation clearly lends itself to the use of uncertainty, this lever is also effective in the "or else" and lost opportunity alternative situations. The certainty of settling on a slightly higher purchase price to ensure the acquisition of a prime parcel of real estate may be preferable to the uncertainty of losing the property. The certainty of concluding a collective bargaining agreement at the cost of concessions, even though distasteful, may be better than the uncertainty associated with prolonged negotiation and the possibility of a strike. These are just recurring illustrations of the core power of uncertainty to influence negotiations—people, corporations, countries all consistently seek certainty over uncertainty. By understanding this basic human trait, you have unlocked one of the true secrets of the negotiation process.

Uncertainty is a state of mind: While uncertainty can be an extremely powerful lever, it does have a potential weakness. Uncertainty is nothing more than a state of mind. Once the unknown is explored or experienced, apprehension and anxiety may diminish substantially. If this occurs, the lever of uncertainty can lose its potency.

For example, a person who has had past dealings with an opponent is in a much better position to predict the opponent's future actions. Familiarity tends to dilute the strength of uncertainty. This is particularly true where the opposing party or lawyer develops predictable patterns you can anticipate.

Insulate yourself from uncertainty: The lever of uncertainty can be used by either party in a negotiation. Consequently, you should always strive to protect your own positions from the uncertainty that can be exerted by your opponents. The most effective way to insulate yourself from uncertainty is to construct a superior knowledge base. This means checking the veracity of your client's statements as well as those of witnesses and opposing parties. It also means being thorough in your research of the law and facts. The first step in taking the offensive is to ensure that your own position is sound and not vulnerable to the leverage of uncertainty.

A basket of cobras: As an illustration, consider the story of an old man and a wicker basket in a remote village of India. The old man approached a group of tourists, telling them that his basket held a secret that could potentially bring great wealth to anyone willing to pay him a dollar. Several of the intrigued tourists pushed forward waving their dollars, which the old man collected. "The basket at my feet contains a large ruby of exceptional clarity," said the old man. "It represents great wealth to anyone who possesses it. But the basket also contains several pieces of polished quartz which are quite pretty, but also quite worthless."

The old man added that he would allow any of the tourists to reach into the basket and remove one stone, provided they were willing to pay him $50 for the privilege. The tourists surged forward with their money.

"Of course it is only fair to warn you that the ruby shares the basket with a family of deadly cobras who are guarding the stone," cautioned the old man. A pause rippled through the crowd as the old man added one final twist. "But then, I could be wrong about the quartz or the snakes or both. Who is willing to find out?"

> Not surprisingly, the old man had no takers. But he still clutched a handful of dollars as the tourists drifted away. The plain wicker basket, his fanciful story, and a large dose of uncertainty had earned him a considerable return.

If you were presented with this offer, how would you respond? Would it make a difference if you were allowed to peek into the basket before handing over your money? Would you be willing to pay for that privilege? And finally, are you certain the ruby and the cobras were in the basket? Only the old man knows for sure. This story illustrates the power that uncertainty exerts in any negotiation.

Practice Tip: You should attempt to inject as much uncertainty as possible into any negotiation situation without jeopardizing or weakening your own position. Conversely, you should maximize and bolster the certainty of your position by means of any favorable facts and circumstances available to you.

---

§ 2.10 Time

Time cannot be seen, heard, or felt. It is parceled out to each of us in identical daily allotments and it dissolves at precisely the same rate. But it doesn't always seem that way. In some situations, time seems to stand still while at other times it hurtles by. This is because it is the perception of time—rather than time itself—that creates these apparent discrepancies. The negotiator who understands and appreciates the subtle variants of time will be in a position to make the clock an ally rather than an enemy.

If uncertainty is the most powerful lever, time is clearly the most subtle. The starting point to understanding the leverage of time is to realize that it is an asset that can be brought to bear to alter the status quo. Like money, manpower, or expertise, the precise amount of time each negotiator brings to the bargaining table is seldom the same.

To illustrate, imagine that each party to a negotiation carries an hourglass of equal size filled with gold dust. At the commencement of bargaining, each negotiator turns over the hourglass. Depending on the volume of gold dust in the hourglass, separate deadlines for a negotiated outcome are set. As the dust dwindles, pressure to act mounts. In many instances, the party with the most time will prevail. Consequently, knowing how much gold dust everyone has becomes extremely important. This is why smart negotiators never reveal their internal deadlines while always seeking to discover their counterpart's end point for resolution.

Because bargaining does not occur in a vacuum, every transaction is necessarily subject to external pressures and circumstances. As time passes, interest rates rise and fall, fiscal years end and begin, markets open and close, evidence to prove alleged facts materializes and dissolves. The list is endless. The more time a negotiator possesses, the more options he has to maneuver. If an opponent is anxious, there is time to wait. If she is angry, there is time to cool off. If expectations are unrealistic, there is time to lower them. Most important, if your bargaining counterpart is under a deadline, there is time to exploit it.

When the choice is to act or to wait, most people wait. Similarly, as a deadline draws closer, most everyone experiences increased pressure to act. These two simple aspects of human nature explain why action occurs at deadlines. In his book *You Can Negotiate Anything*, Herb Cohen made what is probably the most accurate yet basic statement ever made with respect to the effect of time on a negotiation: concessions occur at deadlines.

How many times have you seen the accuracy of this statement borne out? A close analysis of your last half dozen negotiations will probably produce the number six. The lesson is simple. Bring more gold dust to the table, while making sure not to let the other side get a peek at your hourglass. Of course, the circumstances in which you find yourself will not always make this possible. However, you should always strive to gain an edge in time. The results you will be able to achieve will, to a great extent, be tied to your ability to effectively do this. While every negotiation has a beginning and ending, there is no guarantee that the parties will agree on exactly when this occurs. Though many do not realize or appreciate it, the informal period prior to beginning any formal negotiation is crucially important to building rapport, creating trust, and gaining information. The negotiation has clearly begun. The fact that one of the parties does not know or accept this provides you with a decided advantage.

The same is true of the end point of bargaining. A common ploy to spur action is for one of the parties to threaten to walk away from the bargaining table even when there is no intent to cut off talks. This tactic works if the other side believes it to be credible. Sometimes, a party will indeed stage a calculated walk away, fully intending to resume negotiations if the tactic does not succeed. In effect, it is simply a utilization of the leverage of time and uncertainty. Of course, sifting through what is real and apparent is by no means easy, but it is certainly preferable to taking every statement and action by your counterpart at face value.

The best way to protect yourself from this time-based tactic is to develop alternatives to a negotiated outcome. The fact that you have alternatives should be communicated to the other side to project uncertainty. Your read of the opposition should help you distinguish between time-based bluffs and credible threats.

Yet another dimension of the leverage of time has to do with knowing when to make an offer, concede a point, or employ a particular strategy. Lawyers who can consistently make correct timing decisions are rewarded with success at the negotiating table. This is true even though they may not enjoy a superior bargaining position or may be outdone in terms of experience and resources.

To illustrate this aspect of the leverage of time, consider a common problem facing negotiators. At what point should a negotiator make his best offer? Some would contend that, to save time, a fair and generous offer should be made at the outset of a negotiation. While there may be some situations in which this approach might be successful, in most cases such a move would be premature, or ill-advised. The danger lies in the fact that the opposing party is very likely to doubt the sincerity of such an offer. This is especially true if the opponent has prepared for an extended negotiation. An even more dangerous possibility is that the premature offer could be viewed as merely the first of many concessions to come.

By allowing time to pass before making the offer, however, the opposing party's expectations of a drawn-out negotiation are met. While it may seem a waste of time, the process of making opening offers, counteroffers, proposals, and concessions is often necessary. This maneuvering may ultimately lead to the same terms originally offered. However, because more time and effort has been invested, your opponent will likely leave the bargaining table convinced she has extracted the best deal under the circumstances. Your opponent's self-esteem remains intact while you have realized your objective.

PRACTICE TIP: The leverage of time can take many forms. You should analyze every negotiation in terms of the subtle lever of time. Regardless of the circumstances in each case, we urge you to do what is necessary to seize the initiative and turn the clock to your advantage.

---

§ 2.11 Opportunity

Opportunity is the third major leverage device available to influence your opponent's actions. The basis of this lever is to use positive reinforcement to induce action. The key to the leverage of opportunity is to identify those points that you can offer to induce a quid pro quo of greater relative value.

Opportunity is anything that will enhance the other party's position or meet the other party's objectives. The least costly application of the opportunity lever is the apparent concession that, in reality, is of little or no importance to you, but is of value to the person to whom it is offered. The level of effectiveness of this tactic will depend on how successful you are in placing value on the opportunity.

The salary negotiation: The typical salary negotiation between an employer and prospective employee is a common example of how the leverage of opportunity can be used to your advantage. Let us assume that the employer's objective is to obtain the employee's services at the lowest salary possible. Alternatively, the employee is seeking the most attractive compensation package the employer can afford. Further assume that the employer has recently subscribed to a group insurance plan, the cost of which will be minimally affected by the addition of another employee.

Recognizing the prospective employee's desire for fringe benefits such as life and health coverage, the employer offers the insurance plan to the employee in lieu of a salary increase. If the employee agrees, both parties have gained. The opportunity made available to the employee has cost the employer almost nothing in return for a substantial monthly cash savings reflected by the status quo in terms of salary.

On the other hand, the employee has gained a tangible benefit without having to spend one dollar of his salary for insurance premiums. This is a classic example of win-win negotiation occasioned by the leverage of opportunity.

Other applications of the leverage of opportunity may require more substantive concessions. At this point, you must make a judgment as to how much you are willing to give up and how much you stand to receive in return. Only you can make this decision based on complete knowledge of the applicable circumstances and the consequences of your decision.

Of all the levers, opportunity is certainly the most appealing. The promise of mutual gain and emphasis on creative problem solving has made opportunity the driving force behind what is popularly known as win-win negotiation. Though the leverage of opportunity is most frequently used in the business world, it plays a role in every negotiating scenario, including the most acrimonious dispute resolution problems.

Invoking the leverage of opportunity is one of the most effective ways to spur action leading to agreement. And, because of its appeal to the positive, it can make you a hero while helping create an abundance of good will that can yield valuable benefits.

In its most basic form, the leverage of opportunity involves offering something of value to the opposite side in exchange for something you consider to be of greater value. The key to making the leverage of opportunity pay off is to get more than you give. This basic horse-trading concept is exceedingly simple in the abstract, but can get complicated when issues of valuation arise. Fortunately, there are proven techniques to help you make the most of this powerful lever.

Long before the terms reciprocity or quid pro quo ever entered our vocabulary, we learned as youngsters about the leverage of opportunity when we traded baseball cards, marbles, or paper dolls. It is the leverage of opportunity that governs the universal act of swapping half a soda for half a sandwich. The leverage of opportunity is the organizing principle of business and politics and any other pursuit where people help other people to realize their goals by sharing and compromise.

Practice Tip: To maximize the leverage of opportunity, you should never give up anything, no matter how seemingly insignificant, without receiving something in return. The degree of return will be dictated by your negotiating objectives. In some instances, the return will be computed in hundreds of thousands of dollars; in others, it may amount to nothing more than an intangible that can be used later. Never lose sight of the fact that what is insignificant to you may be viewed as something of great value to your opponent.

---

§ 2.12 Sanction

The leverage of sanction is the negative counterpart of opportunity. This lever relies on negative reinforcement to compel or discourage action. The most common example of sanction is the threat. If you don't...we'll strike, we'll sue, we'll take our business elsewhere. The threat is one of the oldest and most commonly used ploys in the long history of negotiation. Moses' admonition to Pharaoh, "Let my people go - or else..." is just one of the countless times it has been used down through the ages. The purpose of the threat is to extract some form of concession through intimidation when reasoned argument doesn't work. While the substance and tone of sanction can provoke vastly different responses, the objective is the same--to achieve compliance. Because of the obvious dangers associated with the use of threats, effective use of this lever requires a high degree of judgment and skill.

Making the leverage of sanction work for you: Several important factors are involved in making the leverage of sanction work for you. First, you must select a sanction that will be effective in moving the other party. There is nothing worse than threatening a sanction only to be met with the response, "Fine, go right ahead." This was never more clearly illustrated than in 1999 when the Major League Baseball Umpires resigned en masse to avoid violating a no-strike clause in their contract while creating leverage based on the "or else" alternative. Unfortunately, the umpires' union misread the effectiveness of their chosen sanction. Major League Baseball gladly accepted their resignations. Not the best use of the leverage of sanction.

Second, you must communicate the sanction. As we have seen, communication can range from ultimatums and threats to more subtle statements based on recognition of a mutual problem. In some instances, the communication can take the form of news leaks, planted information, or veiled references in correspondence allowing the other party to gain access to the information indirectly. This approach is often used in diplomatic channels to head off a publicized confrontation.

Finally, once the potential sanction is communicated, you must be prepared to carry it out or pay the consequences if the other side regards it as a bluff. Credibility is absolutely essential in making effective use of this lever. Always remember that the potential for negative fallout is much greater with this lever than with any of the others. No one likes to be threatened. Because of this, your opponent's principles of integrity and self-respect may overrule reason, causing a confrontation that neither side really wants. This is why care and restraint should be exercised in using the leverage of sanction.

The subtle sanction: A final word of caution should be offered concerning use of the leverage of sanction. Just as it is human nature to seek certainty over uncertainty, it is also clear that nobody likes to be threatened. If someone walks up and pushes you, your natural reaction is to push back. This is how unnecessary fistfights, lawsuits, and even wars come about. Consequently, we urge you whenever possible to use more subtle means that will yield the same results without the negative overtones that a threat will invariably generate.

Lee Iacocca, the UAW, and the subtle sanction: The classic example of effective use of the subtle sanction involved labor negotiations between the economically plagued automobile manufacturer Chrysler and the United Auto Workers. Against a backdrop of declining sales and record losses during the 1982 recession, Lee Iacocca, the colorful president of the Chrysler Corporation, told labor that, unless they were willing to give up benefits earned in previous bargaining sessions, the automaker would be forced to lay off workers and close plants to avoid mounting deficits.

Management's approach was to portray the possibility of layoffs as a legitimate alternative to dealing with a problem over which it had little control. The carmaker was merely communicating a fact of life rather than making a threat generally perceived by the union. Because the problem was real and the promised sanction credible, the workers responded with unprecedented concessions to avoid losing their jobs.

Sanction by example: If you decide to use the leverage of sanction, there are some specific models available to maximize its effectiveness while guarding against the downside. Research indicates that the potency of threats can be enhanced by escalation or consistency. The familiar label by which we all recognize this tactic is that of making an example of something or someone. A highly visible threat made good is extremely effective in creating credibility which can induce, alter, or suppress behavior. Who hasn't experienced the teacher or coach who rants and raves the first day of class or practice to command attention and ensure discipline? As time goes by, the performance is never repeated, but the potential eruption is always in the back of everyone's mind.

Truman and the atomic bomb: President Harry Truman ended World War II with a spectacular use of sanction by example. Faced with the invasion of Japan and an estimated 6 million Japanese and Allied casualties, Truman ordered the flight crew of the Enola Gay to bomb the city of Hiroshima on August 6, 1945. Three days later, Nagasaki was similarly destroyed when Japan refused America's demand to cease hostilities. After the second bomb was dropped, Japan surrendered unconditionally.

Part of the dilemma facing President Truman was the power of the weapon that had been developed by the top secret Manhattan Project. The Japanese were fierce fighters who weren't about to surrender their homeland to their enemies based on perceived propaganda. Because the destructive capability of the atomic bomb was so great, no one who had not seen an actual demonstration could conceive of what it could do to a population center.

Truman has been criticized for not demonstrating the bomb's capability to the Japanese by using a military target. The response is that nothing less than total annihilation of a Japanese city would end the war. As a secondary and arguably even more important consequence, Truman's actions may well have spared the world from destruction by demonstrating the need for a policy of nuclear deterrence.

§ 2.13 How to Combine the Levers to Maximize Your Effectiveness

Most negotiations require using a combination of levers to achieve a client's objectives. It is not uncommon to employ the levers of uncertainty, time, opportunity, and sanction within the framework of a single negotiation. The only restriction on the use of leverage is imagination and resourcefulness. The following example illustrates how the four levers can be used in combination to achieve results.

§ 2.14 The City versus the Transit Workers: The Classic Negotiation Scenario

The following scenario should be familiar to many, especially those who practice in large cities dependent on public mass transit. In this scenario, the transit workers' union has been engaged in protracted negotiations with the city administration over their contract. The union's primary leverage invariably revolves around the threatened sanction of a transit strike that would virtually paralyze the city. This is the classic "or else" alternative wherein the union employs the leverage of sanction to get a better contract with the city. The union times its conduct of the negotiation to ensure that it will go down to the wire. There will be no early solution. The net result of these two factors is the creation of uncertainty in the minds of the public as to whether the city might be brought to a standstill.

Because the city is experiencing severe financial problems at the time of the negotiation, the administration adopts a hard-line stance on any extension of benefits. The city's negotiators decide to fight fire with fire and to allow the negotiation to go down to the wire by standing firm and communicating a willingness to accept a strike. The deadline is set for midnight. At 11:30 p.m., word from bargaining headquarters is that the talks have collapsed and a strike is imminent. Many people go to bed prepared for a long walk to work. The next morning, these same commuters are stunned to learn that the strike has been averted. Both the city and union gave ground at the eleventh hour to reach an agreement. This last-minute compromise is produced by the uncertainty created on both sides.

As the 12:00 a.m. deadline approached, the city and union decided to soften their positions to take advantage of the opportunity of a predictable and certain agreement and to assure the transit workers jobs with liberal benefits in the midst of a troubled economy. On the other side of the table, the city was able to avoid a costly and disruptive strike that would have generated shockwaves far beyond the subway tollbooths to precinct voting booths.

The subway strike that never was is a dramatic yet recurring illustration of how the four levers combine to bring about an eleventh-hour agreement. These same concepts can be applied today to the client files on your desk that lend themselves to a negotiated solution.

3

Personal Negotiating Style: How Leverage Is Used

While the power inherent in leverage constitutes the controlling principles by which all negotiations are conducted, the bottom-line results you are able to achieve will most likely depend on your ability to utilize them. The status quo will always prevail unless and until you take action to transform leverage potential into leverage reality. The more adept you are at recognizing and using leverage, the more successful you will be. This requires an ability to read and interact with people. For this reason, mastering the personal component of the bargaining process is critically important.

§ 3.01 Improve Your Personal Skills to Improve Your Success Level

No two people ever possess precisely the same level of interpersonal skills. Some lawyer-negotiators are simply better with people than others. We all have varying degrees of persuasiveness, resourcefulness, tenacity, and motivation. Despite this fact, there are indeed specific concepts, principles, and patterns that relate to improving your negotiating style. Anyone can improve her basic skills by developing an understanding and appreciation of these factors coupled with a dedicated effort to apply this information every day to the problems and challenges encountered within the context of a law practice.

§ 3.02 The Two Spheres of Personality and Interpersonal Skills

The personal dimension falls into two spheres. One is intangible and subjective by nature. It includes factors such as persuasiveness, resourcefulness, tenacity, and motivation. This intangible dimension also includes traits such as discipline, aspiration, and capacity for risk-taking and confrontation. Some of these traits are highly predictable, while others are less so.

The second sphere consists of basic personality types that all of us were born with and to some extent developed in childhood. These patterns are highly predictable provided you know what to look for when interacting with other negotiators. To help you do just that, we draw on the pioneering work of Dr. William Marston, a psychologist who taught at Columbia University in the 1920s and '30s. Let us begin with the easy part—reading personality types.

§ 3.03 People Are Highly Predictable

Given the billions of people populating the earth and the many different cultures, traditions, and standards of living they experience, it would seem a hopeless task to predict any given individual's behavior. But that is simply not the case. Notwithstanding the infinite variants of the human experience, Dr. Marston's research indicates that people tend to fall into highly identifiable personality groups. When these patterns are understood, they reveal a great deal of information about how people are likely to behave in any given situation. These principles make it possible for anyone to read people and predict an individual's behavior.

When the added advantage of predictability is integrated with the rules of leverage, the odds of achieving consistently successful results as a negotiator are drastically improved. But what are these scientifically verifiable patterns and how can they be recognized in yourself and others? That is the focus of the first part of this chapter.

§ 3.04 Marston's Theory of Behavior

While Freud and Jung were researching the causes of abnormal behavior, Dr. Marston was intent on discovering what motivated normal people to act and react as they do. Marston, who is probably best known for his invention of the lie detector, also created the comic strip "Wonder Woman," which he wrote under a pen name. However, his most enduring legacy was the 1928 publication of *The Emotions of Normal People* in which he articulated his theory of human behavior. According to Marston, people tend to interact with their environment in distinctly similar ways. His research revealed that people's fundamental approach to life is either active or passive. Likewise, people tend to view their environment as being either antagonistic or favorable.

By constructing intersecting lines along these two fundamental axes, four personality quadrants are formed, each of which corresponds to a predictable behavior pattern.

DOMINANCE—Active personalities in an antagonistic setting

INFLUENCE—Active personalities in a favorable setting

STEADINESS—Passive personalities in a favorable setting

COMPLIANCE—Passive personalities in an antagonistic setting

While Marston found that all human beings possess qualities that fall into each of the four quadrants, it became clear that one of the four would predominate, thereby influencing that person's behavior accordingly. He also found that people tended to be much more deliberate in their behavior, thus explaining why only about 20 percent of persons studied could be classified as active. Marston's studies indicated that four in five people preferred incremental change and measured adjustment as a more prudent alternative to proactivity, flux, and change. This helps explain why, in most cases, the status quo tends to change slowly, if at all.

Based on Marston's theory, it is possible to predict general patterns of human behavior by becoming familiar with the traits and patterns that correspond to each quadrant. It is important to note that no personality type is inherently superior or inferior to any other, just different. Each quadrant has its own set of strengths and weaknesses, though people often see their own behavior only in terms of what is considered positive and desirable.

The most important generalization to be drawn from Marston's theory is simply that people are different. Too many negotiators erroneously assume that everyone else shares their perspective, values, and priorities. A foolproof formula for failure is to assume that everyone sees opportunities and problems through your own behavioral filter. Of course, some do and always will. That explains why people are drawn to people like themselves. But it is more likely that you will encounter negotiators who either move too fast or too slowly and who are either too cautious or not cautious enough. The proactive, dominating Hi-D and outgoing, action-oriented Hi-I personalities will tend to view others with more reactive profiles as having too little vision and urgency while being hopelessly immersed in details. Likewise, the more cautious Hi-C and the deliberative Hi-S negotiators are likely to view the Hi-D and Hi-I as being half-cocked, "bulls-in-a-china shop" or grandiose, superficial talkers unwilling or unable to do the hard work necessary to transform ideas into reality.

Test the validity of Marston's theory by seeing if you know anyone who might fit into the following categories.

§ 3.05 Hi-Dominance Personalities

Hi-D people are self-starters who thrive on challenge and competition. They are direct, positive, straightforward people who say what they think, sometimes bluntly. They make decisions quickly and love to be in charge. These self-sufficient individualists seek out adventure and the unusual and are apt to lose interest in anyone or anything that is routine.

While they are demanding of others, they are even tougher on themselves. Hi-D personalities are often high achievers who are best described as being results-oriented and often impatient. In the extreme, they are driven workaholics. A disproportionate number of corporate chief executive officers, military commanders, and litigators share this quadrant.

§ 3.06 Hi-Influence Personalities

Hi-I persons are outgoing, gregarious, and persuasive. They love people and feel very comfortable in one-on-one situations. Optimism and openness are two common traits shared by Hi-I personalities. Because they inherently like and trust people, and want to be liked in return, they sometimes overpromise and tend to trust too much. Hi-I people are natural salespeople who sometimes lose interest in following up once the sale is made. The Hi-I loves being center stage and is drawn to the limelight. This explains why an inordinate number of celebrities and politicians share this quadrant. Former President Clinton is the prototype Hi-I, with all the predictable pluses and minuses. Oprah Winfrey shares this quadrant as well.

§ 3.07 Hi-Steadiness Personalities

The Hi-S is best described as easygoing, even-tempered, and relaxed. Unlike the Hi-D and Hi-I, Hi-S people are low key, undemonstrative people who dislike urgency and change. Although Hi-S people tend to be friendly, they are also possessive about family, belongings, and turf. While they seldom argue or openly criticize, Hi-S people can slow things down in quiet ways if they feel unnecessarily rushed. Actor Jimmy Stewart is the personification of the Hi-S. Former President Ford also falls into the Hi-S quadrant.

§ 3.08 Hi-Compliance Personalities

Hi-Cs are naturally cautious people who proceed in a precise and orderly way. They seek to avoid conflict and antagonism by following established procedures. The Hi-C is the classic detail person who documents everything just in case. These are the people who believe in doing everything "by the book." Unlike the Hi-D, they are reserved and are slow to make decisions. This is the profile of the perfectionist, which explains why an inordinate percentage of concert pianists, chess masters, and certified public accountants are drawn from this quadrant. Not surprisingly, golfer Tiger WOODS is a classic Hi-C.

In the legal field, an inordinate number of tax lawyers, security lawyers, and other attorneys with a detail-oriented practice are

Hi-C. In law school, those members of the law review who are the experts on citation form are most likely members of the Hi-C fraternity. Former President Carter is a Hi-C. While President Carter was often criticized for an inability to make a decision, in actuality, he was constantly refining his choices in an effort to make the very best decision possible.

§ 3.09 Interpreting Behavior

It is relatively easy to identify behavior types when one quadrant is predominant. For instance, it is not difficult to group Hitler, Stalin, and Saddam Hussein as Hi-D personalities to the exclusion of everything else. They all shared a grandiose vision, iron will, paranoia of rivals, and obsession of ruling by edict. This is classic Hi-D behavior in its most extreme form. With each of these dictators, there was a pronounced absence of persuasion, support, or caution. Nothing short of total dominance was acceptable. Luckily, such exaggerated personality extremes are exceedingly rare. Most persons' behavior styles are a composite of Marston's four quadrants. This suggests that the arrangement of a person's Dominant (D), Influential (I), Supportive (S), and Compliant (C), or DISC, factors will further refine his behavioral profile.

People often moderate or mask one trait with another to enhance their effectiveness and personal appeal. For instance, a Hi-D combined with very low I, S, and C fits the profile of the dictator. By understanding these relationships and learning to detect them in ourselves and others, it is possible to refine our ability to read people and make necessary adjustments.

Let us consider some behavioral profiles of two former United States presidents. For each, try to determine the relationship of the various factors. For instance, the Hitler-Stalin-Hussein profile is clearly Hi-D, Low-I, Low-S, and Low-C.

Consider the behavioral profile of President Reagan. Reagan, labeled by the Washington press corps as the Great Communicator, is an interesting composite of Marston factors. If you classified him as a classic Hi-I, you are only partially correct. His Hi-I affability and ability to sell his programs and policies helped mask his Hi-D tendencies. As president, he took every opportunity to push his clearly defined political agenda—conquer communism, drastically cut taxes, and reverse the intrusion of the federal government into the lives of Americans. His uncompromising views, along with his legendary disdain for details, short attention span, and management by delegation underscore a Hi-D personality. Conversely, President Reagan's ongoing assault on liberal policies and his obsession with the Soviet Union are indicative of Low-C, Low-S behavior. President Reagan's genius was an ability to project a Hi-I profile to sell a decidedly Hi-D agenda.

In marked contrast, consider President Nixon. Nixon, a highly competent and pragmatic chief executive, was arguably our most able president in terms of foreign affairs. As with President Reagan, Nixon had a bold vision for the world that allowed him to open China to the West and extricate the United States from the Vietnam War. Despite his immense ability, however, his Hi-D paranoia was eventually his undoing. The Watergate scandal is striking affirmation of the principle that people like people like themselves. The Nixon White House and its alter ego, the Committee to Re-elect the President, was clearly one of the most Hi-D, Hi-C, Low-I, Low-S organizations ever assembled. Haldeman, Ehrlichman, and Mitchell were virtual behavioral clones of their boss.

Consequently, there was no sense of perspective at work. Everything became a political conspiracy and everyone outside the inner circle became a political enemy. With no Hi-I or Hi-S anywhere in sight to moderate the unfavorable filter through which the president and his men viewed the world of politics, it is not at all surprising that Watergate took place. What is even more astonishing is the fact that it was completely unnecessary. No serious student of presidential politics gave George McGovern a realistic chance of beating Nixon, an effective incumbent president. All of this demonstrates the power of behavior to take its own predetermined course in the face of rational arguments to the contrary.

Comparing the relationship of the four quadrants to refine the process of personality prediction is a valuable technique, provided the information is used to its best advantage. The initial objective in every negotiation is to establish the maximum degree of rapport and trust possible. Once this is accomplished, the protective psychological walls that each of us erects when encountering strangers will begin to crumble. Until this happens, it is unrealistic to think that your substantive proposals, no matter how meritorious, will get a fair hearing. Indeed, some people are not trustworthy and should be avoided if possible. However, in most new bargaining relationships, it is erroneous to perceive that your opponent is not trustworthy or that a basic lack of rapport between the parties dooms the relationship from the outset. This is where your knowledge of behavioral patterns becomes an invaluable asset.

Once the critically important prerequisites of rapport and trust have been established, you can begin to use information on behavioral patterns in a tactical sense. For instance, when it comes to bringing a negotiation to closure, you will know that it is best not to push a Hi-S or Hi-C to an early conclusion. Conversely, a Hi-D or Hi-I is likely to lose interest in the deal if the negotiation is drawn out too long. All of this is further complicated by the relationships of the subordinate traits to the predominant trait. Thus, a Hi-D with a healthy dose of Hi-C characteristics will be much more wary of an early conclusion than a Hi-D, Low-C, who will welcome such closure to allow him to focus on the next problem or challenge.

§ 3.10 Using Behavioral Profiles to Negotiate

Assuming you have identified your own profile and that of your negotiation counterpart, how do you make the best use of the information? The first step is to appreciate differences rather than dismissing the profiles of others as being less desirable or somehow inferior to your own. It is important to understand that not everyone sees and experiences life as you do. This becomes even more problematic when negotiators come from different cultural or socioeconomic backgrounds.

Insisting on conformity to your particular behavioral profile is not only unrealistic, it is also dangerous when applied to negotiations. When it comes to bargaining, pushing someone out of her comfort zone is the surest way to kill a deal. Consequently, it is important to construct separate needs profiles for you and your negotiation counterpart. If your personalities fall into the same quadrant, you will probably find it easier to understand each other. However, chances are there will be some degree of discrepancy in your behavioral profiles. The key is to identify the differences and adjust accordingly. The following chart provides a quick reference on how best to bridge the behavioral differences that will inevitably crop up in negotiations.

Hi-Dominance Negotiators

Do:

- *Get right to the point.*
- *Focus the negotiation on objective considerations rather than personal relationships.*
- *Demonstrate exactly why and how your proposal is beneficial to the negotiator.*
- *Emphasize options and results.*
- *Back up your assertions with facts.*
- *Bring your initial presentation to a timely conclusion.*

Do not:

- *Be afraid to use the leverage of time by setting deadlines.*
- *Waste time or go into unnecessary detail.*
- *Overstate or exaggerate.*
- *Appear to be indecisive or unprepared.*
- *Take failure to consider risks and weigh the pros and cons of a proposal as a negative sign.*

Hi-Influence Negotiators

Do:

- *Take time to develop a personal rapport and relationship.*
- *Deal with your negotiation counterpart as an equal.*
- *Be friendly, warm, enthusiastic, and open.*
- *Use the leverage of opportunity.*
- *Ask for input.*
- *Frame conflict-oriented negotiation in terms of joint problem solving.*

Do not:

- *Get down to business immediately.*
- *Be abrupt or curt.*

- *Dominate or monopolize the conversation.*
- *Be put off if they interrupt.*
- *Take lack of concentration or failure to follow up on important facts as a negative sign.*

Hi-Steadiness Negotiators

Do:

- *Take time to establish a comfortable rapport.*
- *Be patient and relaxed in your approach.*
- *Demonstrate your interest by being an attentive listener.*
- *Solicit your counterpart's objectives and concerns.*
- *Stress reliability.*
- *Emphasize your sincerity.*

Do not:

- *Be erratic or impatient.*
- *Be overly aggressive.*
- *Move too fast.*
- *Leave out important details.*
- *Take hesitancy or reluctance to make a decision as a negative sign.*

Hi-Compliance Negotiators

Do:

- *Appeal to logic.*
- *Provide substantiation and documentation to back up your assertions.*
- *Keep negotiations formal and business-like.*
- *Address the details and fine points of your proposal.*
- *Anticipate questions and weaknesses in your proposal.*
- *Make provisions for problems.*

Do not:

- *Be overly familiar or casual in your approach.*
- *Move too fast.*
- *Make statements you cannot substantiate with documentation, statistics, or other forms of demonstrative proof.*

- *Be afraid to go into exacting detail.*
- *Take caution or coolness as a negative sign.*

§ 3.11 Intangible Aspects of Personality

While Dr. Marston's theory is invaluable in predicting behavior, it is a less reliable measure of some of the more intangible aspects of a person's makeup. For traits such as persuasiveness, resourcefulness, tenacity, the capacity for risk taking, and tolerance for confrontation, a DISC analysis is quite helpful. For instance, persuasiveness is an easily recognizable Hi-I trait, whereas the capacity for risk taking and tolerance for confrontation is classic Hi-D behavior. Discipline is the hallmark of a Hi-C.

But what about personality traits that do not lend themselves as readily to objective measurement, such as reciprocity, motivation, resourcefulness, and aspiration? Here, observation and personal knowledge are more important factors in reading people. We refer to these more subtle traits as intangible connectors. They, too, play a key role in any negotiation. For many of these concepts, we are indebted to the pioneering work of Dr. Robert Cialdini and his book *Influence: The Psychology of Persuasion,* first published in 1984.

The Intangible Connectors: When the intangible connectors are coupled with Marston's four basic personality types, a more detailed profile of an individual negotiator begins to emerge. This profile helps you understand and better appreciate the motivations and behavior of your bargaining counterpart.

The connectors become important when the personality types of the negotiators are aligned. It is only natural that negotiations will flow more smoothly when there is mutual trust and understanding between bargainers who genuinely like each other.

The intangible connectors are much more important when DISC profiles are in opposition to each other. For example, consider a demanding, impatient Hi-D dealing with a detail-oriented Hi-C with little sense of urgency. It is quite likely that conflicts will develop that might endanger the prospects of a successful negotiation. In extreme situations, the differences can so polarize the parties that reaching an agreement is almost impossible. In situations such as these, you may find yourself seeking ways to bridge the interpersonal gulf and connect with the other side. This is where the intangible connectors can prove especially helpful.

Let's take a quick look at the intangible connectors.

Similarity: We have already alluded to this factor in our discussion on Marston's theory of behavior. As noted, people are drawn to people like themselves. Consequently, it is always easier to establish a rapport with a negotiator who shares your DISC profile.

As an example, consider individuals at a party. Hi-Is invariably find each other in the first five minutes, establish an instant rapport, and dominate the conversation for the rest of the evening. At a social gathering, the Hi-I is the "life of the party." The same is true of Hi-Ds, though to a lesser extent. At the party, the Hi-D will gravitate to other Hi-Ds to express strongly held views on a wide range of subjects. What ensues will likely range from a spirited debate to an argument. If there is only one Hi-D in the room, he will most likely be the one engaging the others in a discussion on politics or religion.

Meanwhile, Hi-S partygoers tend to form an attentive audience for the extroverted Hi-Is and opinionated Hi-Ds. The Hi-Cs, on the other hand, will stand back and observe the more gregarious Hi-Is or Hi-Ds, often becoming annoyed or embarrassed at their behavior. If alcohol is being served, all of these behaviors will be exaggerated in direct proportion to the amount consumed. The next time you're at a party, try to spot the various behavior types.

While similar DISC profiles make it easier for negotiators to hit it off, your knowledge of DISC characteristics provides valuable clues about how to close any rapport gaps that might exist at the outset of a bargaining relationship.

While a compatible DISC analysis illustrates the rapport-building principle of similarity, there are countless other applications. Any element of similarity between people or groups represents a basis on which to establish a level of personal connection from which a spirit of trust and cooperation can grow. Mutual acquaintances or friendships, similar cultural backgrounds, the same alma mater, and shared political affiliations are only a few common connectors that illustrate the principle of similarity. The key to making this principle work for you is to search out those common elements at the outset of any bargaining relationship. The benefit of doing so will become more apparent as the relationship grows and the ultimate deal is struck.

Physical Attractiveness: One of the more subtle connectors suggested by Cialdini is physical attractiveness. His research revealed that physically attractive people tend to receive preferred treatment in such diverse settings as school, business, and even the legal system. One experiment showed that handsome men convicted of crimes received substantially lighter sentences than less attractive men. Another study indicated that in damage suits based on negligence, physical attractiveness of the plaintiff and defendant played a major role in the amount of the damage award.

While we have no control over our physical attributes, we can maximize our appearance through good grooming and conservative dress. These are potential connectors that can make an enormous difference in a negotiation's final outcome.

Recognition: We have all heard the old saying, "Flattery will get you nowhere." Nothing could be further from the truth. Everyone wants to be liked and appreciated for who they are and what they do; conversely, no emotionally healthy individual likes to be criticized or ignored. Keep in mind, however, that people can see through insincerity. Empty flattery is nothing more than blatant manipulation and it can frequently backfire. But genuine recognition can go a long way in forging rapport with your negotiating partner.

Reciprocity: Reciprocity, according to Cialdini, obligates us to give something back to the person who has given us something first. To illustrate, consider the following real life example involving one of the authors. On a shopping trip to Bangkok, he entered a small shop on a side street. As he entered the shop, the salesperson immediately greeted him with a smile and an invitation to look around. A few minutes later, another employee offered him a complimentary soft drink. It even had ice which was particularly welcome on a hot, humid day in Thailand. With that small gesture, he was hooked. Not only did he have positive feelings about his hosts, but he also felt obligated to make a purchase. In the end, he bought much more than he intended. He was on the receiving end of the principle of reciprocity, though he wasn't complaining. In fact, the next time he was in Bangkok, he planned to make it a point to give the store some more business!

This same principle has wide application at the negotiation table. The gift can be as intangible as a smile or as tangible as a get-acquainted lunch at which you pick up the tab. The key is to act first by extending yourself as a show of good faith. As with the soft drink with ice, it was the gesture as much as the drink. But then again, it really was hot that day in Bangkok.

Conditioning and Association: When forging the all-important connection with your negotiating counterparts, much of your success will depend on how you characterize your role. This is especially true where the prospective negotiation involves potentially unpleasant or negative overtones. This principle can be illustrated by a real life negotiation when I was serving as a studio executive for Columbia Pictures Television Group in Burbank, Calif.

One of the studio's more successful, long-running series had finally run its course and had been cancelled by the network. As is standard in the business, the studio was a joint venturer in the series with an independent production company. My assignment was to oversee shutting down the production and to inventory all props, sets, and equipment belonging to the studio. My initial phone call to the show's producer to discuss shutting down the production was met with not so veiled hostility. The producer was understandably upset that his series had been canceled. Although I had nothing to do with the show's demise, I was nevertheless viewed as the enemy who was being sent to confiscate the producer's personal property before kicking him off the lot.

Because perception is reality, I had a problem. Legally I had the authority to do my job with or without the producer's cooperation. From a practical standpoint, however, a heavy-handed approach would make my task infinitely more difficult. Using the principle of conditioning and association, I had to convince the producer that I was not just another studio "suit," but rather an empathetic ally there to insure an orderly transition. This required several personal meetings to win over the producer before we ever got down to labeling the first production prop. Over time, the producer came to see me not as a faceless studio hatchet man but as an understanding individual who was trying to help make a tough situation more bearable. Once the shift in association was accomplished, the assignment came off without a hitch. More important, I learned the value of establishing trust at the outset of a negotiating relationship.

> ***Anger—The Major Disconnector:*** Anger is the major disconnector of negotiations at every level. When people become angry, communications break down and negotiations come to a halt.

Effective negotiators learn to harness this emotion in themselves and to exploit it in their opponents. Anger has certain predictable characteristics. Once you recognize and understand them, you can use this knowledge to your advantage.

While anger typically manifests itself in a loud voice, harsh words, or threatening gestures, these manifestations are not the source. Understanding the origin of someone's anger is critical to overcoming it.

Anger generally occurs when a person feels he has been wronged. Assaulting a person's convictions, beliefs, reference groups, or family can cause anger. Regardless of your intent, if the other person feels that you have assaulted him, he will become angry. While you cannot control feelings, you can control the nature of the perceived threat by depersonalizing your words as much as possible to avoid tripping the anger wire.

If anger is unleashed, it is helpful to understand its cycle. Anger is short-lived. Thomas Jefferson advised that when angry, count to 10 before you do anything, and when very angry, count to 100.

We have all responded to someone during the heat of anger only to regret our words later. Once you gain control over your emotions, you become a much better negotiator.

Another stage of the anger cycle is the heightened state of excitement which produces a rush of adrenaline and causes a temporary confidence. But, like drugs, it eventually wears off. Once the feeling of confidence subsides and reality sets in, the angry person usually starts to do damage control.

In summary, the key things to remember about anger are that it is triggered by a personal attack, it is temporary, and it produces a feeling of heightened confidence. Remember these anger antidotes:

- Never mix harsh words with a harsh tone.
- Never attack the person; attack the problem.
- Never negotiate with an angry opponent.

§ 3.12 Motivation

The starting point of every successful negotiation is a motivated person unwilling to live with the status quo. Having the motivation to achieve tangible results at the bargaining table can fuel lawyers and their clients with the initial impetus to approach a negotiation in the comprehensive manner that we advocate. It can provide courage to overcome obstacles as a way of changing the status quo for the better. It breeds optimism in difficult times. No matter the number and extent of problems confronting you, few situations are hopeless. A motivated and committed negotiator will have the inner strength to recognize this and stay the course even in the face of adversity.

§ 3.13 Aspiration

Chester L. Karrass was one of the first negotiation theorists to explore the relationship between aspiration and bargaining success. He concluded that one's level of tangible success at the negotiation table corresponded directly to the negotiator's aspiration level. Nearly a decade later, Karrass's hypothesis was borne out by empirical research. Gerald Williams, a law professor at Brigham Young University, conducted an experiment to measure aspiration level. Williams randomly selected and matched pairs of Iowa attorneys to negotiate a settlement to a hypothetical legal problem. The attorneys were given precisely the same objective information. Each pair of attorneys negotiated the problem independently from the others. When the results were tabulated Williams was surprised to find a settlement range that extended from a low of $15,000 to a high of $95,000. The experiment bears out the importance aspiration plays in the final outcome of the problem.

Based on work done by Karrass and Williams, we have independently sought to verify the role of aspiration in negotiation by informally monitoring law students as they negotiate hypothetical problems and exercises. Invariably, those students who make higher initial demands reach higher final settlements. Conversely, students who ask for less consistently get less at the negotiation table. This has proven to be the case even after having discussed the role of aspiration in class prior to assigning problems. Our experience with aspiration confirms the validity of the work done by Karrass and Williams. It also suggests that one's basic aspiration level is largely predetermined by one's personality profile, life experiences, and other factors.

Is there any way to predict or measure one's aspiration level? According to Karrass, aspiration is determined in one of three ways: (1) one's individual past performance or experience; (2) past performance or experience of a peer group; or, (3) on the basis of performance or experiences of groups to which the negotiator would like to belong. This would indicate that part of preparation for negotiation would be to investigate your counterpart's past levels of aspiration and performance as well as her associations.

While this would undoubtedly provide valuable insight into what might be expected, it does not tell the entire story. The ability to predict aspiration can also be tied to Marston's theory. Obviously, people's aspirations are in large part determined by what they view as important. To the extent that one's behavioral profile reveals one's priorities, it can help predict one's aspiration level. This in turn allows one to prepare and adjust accordingly.

§ 3.14 Self-Confidence and Your Negotiating Style

The final intangible transcends negotiation. In the end, it has a direct effect on everything we do every day of our lives. This intangible is self-confidence.

Each of us possesses varying degrees of self-confidence. Self-confidence stems from our ability to triumph over a variety of challenges, problems, and obstacles over a lifetime. Every time we succeed, our confidence is bolstered; every time we fail, our confidence is diminished. With each success, we look for greater challenges and new successes; with each failure, we seek to avoid future challenges for fear of failure. This up-and-down process explains why one's own confidence level is always undergoing change. The older we get, the less dramatic and pronounced the changes. By the time we reach adulthood, much of our confidence level is fixed. Consequently, most of our adult decisions that are affected by self-confidence tend to be consistent and usually predictable.

In the context of a negotiation, the self-confidence of the negotiator will reveal a great deal about how a person is likely to act and react. Use of leverage and response to pressure will be affected by this personality characteristic. A person with a relatively low level of self-confidence will likely have lower expectations and will take fewer risks. As a general rule, he will make more concessions and will be more easily intimidated. On the other hand, the self-confident negotiator will expect more, risk more, be less likely to compromise, and be better able to combat superior leverage.

§ 3.15 Self-Confidence Is Only One Component of Your Negotiating Style

Self-confidence is only one component of many that combine to shape and mold an individual's personal negotiating style. Other important factors include socioeconomic background, intelligence, education, parental and peer relationships, cultural, geographic and religious background, individual experiences, and personal temperament. All of these factors translate into a distinct personality that in turn will determine your specific negotiating style. Your negotiating style remains more or less constant over a lifetime. The older you get, the more difficult it is to change.

§ 3.16 Recognizing Your Weaknesses Will Help Make You a Stronger Negotiator

Regardless of how skillful you might be in terms of personal negotiating style, it is only human nature to want to improve. An understanding of your own particular motivations, insecurities, and values is a logical starting point for improvement. While recognition alone will not cure bad habits or eliminate weaknesses, it will help to prevent you from rationalizing shortcomings or placing the blame on more convenient and less personal reasons.

§ 3.17 Overcoming Shyness: An Example of How to Take Charge of Yourself

A common problem hindering effective interaction between people is shyness. When this trait is manifested in a negotiation, it can result in a number of potentially negative consequences. As a result of shyness, the negotiator tends to avoid confrontation, makes unnecessary concessions, and fails to exploit negotiating alternatives that require initiating contact with others. This naturally will impede a negotiator's ability to achieve successful settlements and agreements. Once the negotiator is willing to acknowledge her shyness and the fact that it is causing her to be less effective at the bargaining table, she is in a better position to deal with the problem. By making a conscious effort to relate to people rather than avoiding them, one can begin to overcome shyness.

Asserting control over a problem is rarely cost-free. The price is usually paid in terms of an increased discomfort level. However, as with anything, the discomfort decreases each time the problem is confronted until a point is reached at which the problem ceases to exist. Over the long run, the negotiator's personal approach and negotiating style are altered for the better as a result of a heightened level of awareness of the factors that help shape his actions.

§ 3.18 No One Said It Was Easy

Recognizing a weakness and doing something about it is seldom easy. Many influences and values are so deeply etched on our personalities by a lifetime of reinforcement that it is extremely difficult to deal with them at all. However, numerous habits, patterns, and attitudes that contribute to our personal effectiveness can be improved or altered simply by making the effort to understand them. Regardless of the particular trait you would like to alter or improve, this is the first step. Being honest with yourself and being persistent in dealing with it is the only way you can improve your effectiveness at the negotiating table and beyond.

Circumstance: Despite your ability to understand yourself and your negotiation counterpart and no matter how prepared and determined you might be, there is a final intangible factor that may well be beyond your control. This is the variable of circumstance. All experienced attorneys know that the first rule of practicing law is that one must take their clients as they find them. How often have we all uttered the familiar refrain, "If you had only come to see me earlier, we could have easily avoided this problem." But unfortunately, this often doesn't occur. Consequently, negotiators trying to make a deal or resolve a dispute find themselves in situations over which they have little or no control.

When this is the case, we advise you to accept the hand you were dealt and move on to the best of your ability. This requires you to develop a sense of realism that your client might not share. Wishful thinking in the face of harsh reality can only lead to futile and even disastrous consequences. It is for precisely this reason that you must find a way to develop a bond of trust with your client that will allow him to tell you everything; the good, the bad, and the ugly. You must also be able to persuade your client to accept the reality of the circumstances surrounding his situation and then proceed accordingly.

The good news about circumstance is that it can just as easily work to your advantage, provided you make a thorough and realistic appraisal of the situation. The starting point in making the best out of the intangible of circumstance is to heed the aphorism that "History repeats itself - but never exactly." This allows you to look at past cases, closed files, and even world history as a source of guidance in situations where existing or developing circumstances made all the difference in a negotiation's outcome.

To illustrate, just imagine that you were a real estate investor living in San Francisco in 1906. Further assume that you had negotiated an agreement to purchase three downtown office buildings and that the deal was set to close on April 20. San Francisco was hit by an 8.3 earthquake accompanied by severe aftershocks on April 18 and 19 which destroyed much of the city. Would this unforeseen circumstance drastically alter your fortunes and what would the legal implications be? How would you respond?

The point is that circumstances change all the time. Whether it takes the form of a natural disaster like Hurricane Katrina or the collapse of the housing and stock markets in 2008, the deal which you are negotiating can change in the blink of an eye, sometimes for better and sometimes for worse. To the extent possible, allow for potential change in circumstances. If change creates potential opportunities, look for and take advantage of them. On the other hand, make provisions for a negative change in existing conditions by purchasing insurance or insisting on provisions in the negotiation that would shield your client from disaster, to the extent that is possible. Unfortunately, sometimes it isn't, but that shouldn't keep you from making educated guesses about the future and from acting accordingly.

Putting it All Together: Integrating the tangible and intangible factors of personality with the concepts of motivation, aspiration, and circumstance will often determine the outcome of any given negotiation. Despite the unavoidable difficulty and periodic frustration inherent in this task, the key to success is to incorporate these factors in your overall negotiation plan. The next chapter provides a step by step process for doing this. Just make sure that the foregoing is factored into your bargaining blueprint. And finally, when inevitable frustration and pressure begin to manifest themselves, be secure in the knowledge that most negotiators don't spend adequate preparation time on these tangible and intangible factors. In fact, many never even address them.

4

Preparation: The Essential Ingredient for Success

§ 4.01 Introduction

Good negotiators, like good lawyers, are prepared. They know where they are going and how they will get there. As any successful lawyer will tell you, superior preparation can often spell the difference between winning and losing, especially in hard-fought, complicated cases. The same is true with negotiation. Even in the simplest matters, preparation is the element that allows you to weave relevant information and applicable negotiating principles into a winning result.

Unfortunately, preparation takes time, a commodity that is at a premium in any busy law office. However, the alternative to spending the necessary time to prepare is generally reflected by a losing performance, both in the courtroom and at the bargaining table.

Practice Tip: When it comes to preparation, there is only one choice for successful negotiators. Do it. That means taking the necessary time to ensure that your assumptions and information are accurate, thorough, and in sufficient detail to allow you to take charge of a negotiation. This is the only way to avoid being dragged along by circumstances, the opposing lawyer, or both.

While all will readily concede preparation takes time, too many lawyers unnecessarily reinvent the wheel in the name of taking time to prepare. On the other end of the spectrum, others never get around to inventing the wheel in the first place. Both of these preparation problems are unnecessary. This chapter is devoted to helping you streamline your preparation, to make the most of the time you have and, above all, to help you know exactly where you are going and precisely how you are going to get there.

§ 4.02 Taking a Long-Range View of Preparation Will Pay Dividends

Preparation actually involves two distinct issues. One relates to the short term of getting ready to negotiate, setting goals, adopting strategies, and selecting tactics. The other relates to a more long-range, big-picture approach that will affect every negotiation, every file, and every client in your practice. Unfortunately, many effectiveness problems experienced by lawyers relate to a narrow view that some lawyers have of preparation. There is a great deal more to preparation than just gathering facts about a particular personal injury claim or formulating a list of demands in a property settlement negotiation.

Besides these essential short-term considerations, important long-range aspects of preparation that relate to image, interpersonal skills, goal formation, and strategic planning should be carefully considered and addressed. Many of these are extremely powerful, although often subtle, making it easy to overlook, minimize, or dismiss their importance. Successful negotiators recognize the importance of these long-range aspects of preparation and emphasize the role they play in their overall approach to negotiation. If you are not dealing with them, now is a good time to start.

Many of the elements we will discuss are long-term in nature and are not usually considered under the topic of preparation. Nonetheless, dealing effectively with each of them will pay enormous long-term dividends. While some might feel that a discussion of the overarching issues related to long term preparation might better be covered in a book on law office management, our experience counsels otherwise.

§ 4.03 The Role People Skills Play in Successful Negotiation

Lawyers have been led to believe that just because they hold a license to practice law they are also expert interviewers, counselors, and negotiators. This is simply not true. In actuality, because we are all busy to the point of being overwhelmed, few lawyers set aside the time to fully develop a comprehensive approach to dealing with people beyond acknowledging that it is important. Often, little or no thought is given to why one deals with people in a certain way and whether there might be a more efficient way of achieving the same results. Settlements that are less than satisfactory, contracts drawn with too many concessions, and clients who never come back reflect this shortsighted approach.

Unfortunately, in an overwhelming number of instances, the failure to operate at optimum effectiveness results from a lack of developing interpersonal skills. Fortunately, once these skills are learned, they become automatic. The positive effects they engender inure to your benefit throughout your professional life.

> ***Practice Tip:*** A conscious effort to develop interpersonal skills should be part of your long-range view of preparation.

§ 4.04 The Power of the First Impression

We all know from experience the power that first impressions play in our dealings with others. The first impression warrants special significance whenever lawyers become involved. Clients and other lawyers often carry preconceived notions about a particular lawyer into the first encounter with that person. Preliminary impressions will either strengthen one's positive perceptions about the lawyer or will raise and reinforce doubts about her. A favorable first impression will get a negotiation off on the right track and keep it there.

Appearance: Before you say a word, your appearance will generate signals to a client or opposing lawyer. As common sense and experience demonstrate, a smiling and energetic face will go a long way in projecting a favorable image. Lawyers who have pleasant personalities and maintain a positive mental attitude just naturally attract clients and project positive impressions to other lawyers. While this may seem elementary, take time to observe your initial reaction to others and your basis for those reactions. You are likely to be surprised by the intensity of your impressions, both positive and negative. Keep in mind that this process is going on constantly with others you encounter—the only difference is that you are the one they are sizing up.

Dress: Dress conservatively and tailor your wardrobe to the occasion. Continuity of image is best served for men by the dark blue or gray suit, solid white or blue dress shirt with a button-down collar, conservative regimental tie, and dark shoes and belt. For women, a no-nonsense blue or gray suit with a white silk blouse is always appropriate. Interestingly enough, there are some wardrobe authorities who draw distinctions between when the lawyer should wear a blue or gray suit and when an Ivy League or regimental tie should be worn. These clothing experts make a good case for varying the color of clothing to make different psychological impressions on juries.

Given the trend toward more casual dress, it may well be necessary to take local customs into account. While we generally stand by the foregoing advice on dress, it should be taken within the context of the realities around you. For instance, many of the new economy firms across the country have adopted a greatly relaxed standard of dress that comports with their 20-something "dot com" clientele. When it comes to the issue of dress, the worst thing is to exclude yourself by not fitting in.

§ 4.05 The Power of Personal Perceptions

In Chapter 3, we discussed the importance of reading people, using the pioneering work of Dr. Marston. In addition to one's basic behavioral profile, it is equally important to recognize and react to the perceptions and needs of clients, adversaries, and opposing lawyers. This is analogous to a quarterback reading the opposing team's defense and calling the next play accordingly.

Every lawyer, judge, or client has certain preconceived impressions about lawyers in general and you in particular. In most cases, these perceptions will be a jumble of feelings, emotions, and expectations—some valid, others fictitious. Regardless of the validity of these preconceived perceptions, you have no choice but to deal with them. The more you are able to measure up and reinforce positive perceptions while dispelling negative ones, the more satisfactorily a given transaction will go.

Once the opposing lawyer determines that you are competent and honest, she will naturally drop a certain degree of guarded reserve. This makes any working relationship much easier and more productive. Therefore, it is important to survey the opposing lawyer's perceptions about you and then respond with the right signals. Unfortunately, too many lawyers miss this point altogether. They flounder through a negotiation wondering why rapport never materialized. There is usually a reason. It is much better to discover that reason before irreparable damage is done to your prospects for a successful outcome.

§ 4.06 The Power of Natural Advantage

Because of your status as a lawyer, you enjoy certain natural advantages in dealing with people, especially clients, on a professional basis. If you are to negotiate effectively on behalf of a client, it is essential that your relationship with the client be based on confidence, trust, and open communication. Your natural advantage can help create such a relationship.

One advantage of being a lawyer is that your clients voluntarily seek your advice. This means that your client has made an independent decision that he has a problem and needs professional help. Under these circumstances, the client is much more likely to tell you what is on his mind and to listen to what you have to say.

Practice Tip: Your words, actions, and demeanor should be calculated to reinforce the fact that the client has made the right decision in coming to you. You should also reassure the client that you are interested in what he has to say and encourage him to confide in you regarding all relevant details of the problem. This can result in instant, positive rapport while ensuring that you are getting a complete picture of the client's particular situation.

Take charge of the initial meeting: Nonlawyers generally regard lawyers as authority figures who possess superior intelligence, knowledge, and experience. Additionally, most lawyers are perceived as being organized and accustomed to taking control of problem situations. For these reasons, clients are much more apt to let you set the pace. This means you have a head start in controlling the relationship. It is important that you take advantage of this opportunity by taking charge of the initial meeting. Do not wait for the client to set the tone of the relationship. If you do, you most likely will appear to be weak and indecisive.

Be objective: Because you are representing the interests of others, you have the advantage of detached objectivity that generally is not enjoyed by your client. If you allow yourself to become too emotionally involved in your client's problem, you run the risk of losing this natural advantage. While it is important that you be committed to your client's cause, don't become emotionally caught up with your client's problem to the extent that you do not look at the weaknesses of her position, or fail to verify the accuracy of her story.

Be skeptical: Lawyers are trained to be skeptics. You should never accept everything someone tells you at face value. It is your job to satisfy yourself as to the accuracy and validity of a given statement or proposition. This skepticism is a decided advantage when representing the overly optimistic business client who wants to dwell on the positive while ignoring the pitfalls of a deal or an intimidated civil or criminal defendant who is convinced that only the worst will come to pass.

There are situations when you can become too devoted to your client's cause. When this happens, the tendency is to make the client's problems your own. The case becomes a personal crusade, causing the lawyer to lose sight of the client's concerns, needs, and objectives. Beating the other lawyer becomes the sole objective and criterion for success. Inflexibility and reticence may replace calculated objectivity, resulting in decisions based on emotion rather than reason. You should take great care to avoid these all too human tendencies.

§ 4.07 The Power of Effective Communication

Whether you are trying to advise a client, solicit information from a witness, or persuade another lawyer to accept a negotiation point, a key to your level of effectiveness is your ability to communicate.

Illustrations of faulty communication are abundant. One notable example revolves around a foreign marketing campaign conducted several years ago by a major American automobile manufacturer. The automaker sought to create a demand for its midsize Nova automobile in several Latin American countries. The Nova had achieved a high degree of popularity in the United States. In light of this success, company executives reasoned that it could do equally well in foreign markets.

The Nova was introduced to Spanish-speaking consumers, who overwhelmingly rejected the product. The reason for the failure? Very simple: In Spanish the phrase "no va" means "no go." A simple breakdown in communication had a direct and substantial negative impact on bottom-line results. The same danger is ever present in the sphere of legal negotiation.

§ 4.08 Effective Communication Is Simply a Matter of Preparation

Effective communication, whether oral or written, requires a great deal of care, preparation, and practice. While the entire process of effective communication could fill a separate volume, the following principles should serve as a foundation for your communication skills.

Be precise: We all know the dangers of a vague or ambiguous clause in a contract or will. The true intent of the parties is obscured or blurred because of imprecise expression. This same danger exists within the context of a negotiation. A solution to a negotiation problem is only as good as your ability to express it and have it understood. This is why precision in word selection, and care in how those words are presented, is vitally important.

Keep it simple: Verbosity seems to be an occupational hazard for lawyers. It should not be. You can avoid this stumbling block by being simple, direct, and to the point. Too many lawyers have a deadly fear of periods and two-syllable words.

PRACTICE TIP: After you have said what you have to say as succinctly as you know how, stop.

Be an active listener: How many times have you been introduced to someone only to find that you do not remember his name five minutes later? Why does this happen? Possibly because you were introduced to Yanokan Czintrolansk or Machenshu D. Abundanutitus, but more probably because you failed to listen actively to the other person's name when the formal introduction was made.

Real listening requires disciplined concentration. This can prove to be a considerable challenge, especially when the person you are listening to is the personification of rambling imprecision and chronic verbosity. Any lawyer knows from experience that a number of clients and too many lawyers tend to fit this description. This is why it is doubly important to develop good listening habits that will allow you to ferret out relevant information and ask probing questions designed to cut through the verbiage and get to the problem. Sustained active listening is by no means easy, but it is essential to your success as a negotiator.

Watch your interruptions: There is a natural tendency to interject a comment or idea without letting the person who is talking complete her statement. As a result, we spend more time preparing our own rejoinders than we do listening to what the person on the other side of the conversation has to say. Because you are not hearing a portion of the message, this opens the door to misunderstandings rather than to solutions.

Practice Tip: Once you adopt and practice these basic principles of human interplay and communication, they will become automatic. The advantages to be gained will serve you for a lifetime.

§ 4.09 Getting Ready to Negotiate: A Systematic Approach to Preparation

The preceding factors tend to have an indirect, long-term effect on all negotiations. Often these factors are scarcely noticed and tend to work in extremely subtle ways. In contrast, preparing to negotiate in the short-term will have a direct impact on the negotiating process. This section is primarily concerned with formulating realistic goals as well as selecting the proper strategy and tactics to achieve the desired results.

§ 4.10 Find Out What Your Client Wants from a Negotiation

The concept of leverage proceeds from one's self-interest. Consequently, the first area of inquiry for all lawyer-negotiators is identifying the client's self-interest in very specific, concrete terms. In other words, what *exactly* does your client want from a particular negotiation? Unfortunately, determining the client's true wishes can often be difficult and, in some cases, a never-ending process. Nonetheless, the heart of any negotiation centers on getting the client what she wants. Thus, your first task is to obtain a highly specific answer to that question.

§ 4.11 Categorize Your Client's Objectives

To help categorize your client's objectives, divide his goals into three types: deal points, secondary points, and trade points.

"Deal points" are those points the client *absolutely must have* to make the negotiation worthwhile. Put another way, if the client cannot obtain the deal point(s), there is no compelling reason to pursue the negotiation. It would be better to move to the next best alternative or to accept the status quo.

Because a deal point merits the highest priority, there will be very few of them in any negotiation. You will probably not want to compromise your deal points. If you are willing to compromise a deal point, there is a very good chance that it is probably not a deal point at all, but rather, a secondary point. For all these reasons, when it comes to classifying objectives, pay special attention to what is and is not a legitimate deal point because it will affect everything you do once the negotiation begins.

"Secondary points" involve goals and objectives that are important but not necessarily vital to the client. A secondary point can be compromised if necessary to obtain a deal point. Conversely, a deal point should never be compromised.

"Trade points" are everything else in the negotiation. Trade points can range from lower priority goals the client would like to achieve, but that will not play a substantial role in the overall success or failure of the final agreement, to matters that have little or no value to your client, but could have great value to your bargaining counterpart.

From a tactical standpoint, trade points are extremely important to a skillful negotiator. While having little worth to your client, they can often represent valuable secondary or deal points in your opponent's mind. The best application of the leverage of opportunity is to use these trade points as concessions or as a quid pro quo for secondary or deal points your counterpart would be willing to relinquish.

§ 4.12 Two Key Questions That Will Reveal Your Client's Real Objectives

During the initial client interview, you should give your client the opportunity to tell the complete story before you start addressing specific issues through questioning. Once you have elicited all the relevant facts, you should focus on your client's specific goals. This information can be obtained by asking two questions during the interview:

1. If you could have everything you want in this negotiation, what would you desire in the final agreement?
2. If everything goes against us in this negotiation, what would be the very least you would accept to conclude an agreement?

Based on the answers your client gives you, fill in the form below accordingly.

Deal Points

1. ______________________________

2. ______________________________

3. ______________________________

Secondary Points

1. ______________________________

2. ______________________________

3. ______________________________

Trade Points

1. ____

2. ____

3. ____

4. ____

§ 4.13 How to Prepare Your Negotiating Strategy

The next step in the preparation process is selecting the particular strategy that will be followed throughout the negotiation. Strategy decisions should answer the question, "How will I achieve my client's objectives?" For instance, in a personal injury case, some lawyers adopt a strategy of filing the lawsuit before beginning negotiations. Others employ just the opposite approach by immediately entering into negotiations and using the threat of a lawsuit as leverage throughout the discussions. Strategy is the direction in which one moves toward one's goal. The actual mechanics of taking specific action will be embodied in the tactics you employ to reach your bargaining objectives.

Strategy will be determined by a number of factors, including the negotiating styles of you and your adversary, specific facts and circumstances, and relative leverage positions. You should analyze and catalogue all of these factors. Essential facts and leverage positions should be simplified and put in outline form. This visual overview will be a great aid when developing an overall strategy and specific tactics.

Consider asking variations of these key questions to determine the client's real goals. Repetition is the key to gaining this important information. The client's response to these questions will provide you with a negotiating target. If your client's goals are unrealistic, you can take the necessary action to reduce her expectation level. Reference to unfavorable statutes, case law, verdict expectancy statistics, and your overall judgment as to your client's chances for success can help in adjusting her goals to a more realistic level.

If this is necessary, it is especially important to do it at the outset of the lawyer-client relationship, before your client develops an unrealistic, rigid, and uncompromising mindset. On the other hand, if your client has adopted a low expectation level, you may want to reinforce this position to insulate her from possible disappointment. If it turns out that the final result exceeds your client's expectations, all the better.

After a thorough interview and analysis of your client's response to the key questions mentioned above, the three categories of goals will emerge. You can then proceed to the next step of goal formulation.

§ 4.14 Goal Formulation

Once you have identified the client's goals, you are in a position to organize them in the order of importance.

Strategy is important in negotiation because it gives shape and direction to the isolated moves you will make. Strategic planning facilitates tactical decision-making designed to move you to your final objective. On the other hand, negotiating without strategy usually results in random selection of tactics that bring hit-and-miss results. For instance, in the personal injury example above, the lawyer who withheld filing suit as long as negotiations were ongoing would not threaten to file suit at every impasse during the negotiation. Instead, the subtle threat of suit would be interwoven in the entire pattern of the negotiation. On the other hand, lawyers adopting the "sue now, talk later" approach are in a better position to use the threat of suit in the initial meeting with the opposition.

§ 4.15 How to Size Up the Opposing Party

To a great extent, strategy and tactics will be determined by your opposing party's objectives. You should accumulate sufficient information in your opening moves to identify or at least shed light on your opponent's goals. This information should then be charted as follows:

Opponent's Deal Points

1. ______________________________

2. ______________________________

3. ______________________________

Opponent's Secondary Points

1. ______________________________

2. ______________________________

3. ______________________________

Opponent's Trade Points

1. ______________________________

2. ______________________________

3. ______________________________

After completing an analysis of your opponent's goals, you should compare the objectives of all the parties in the negotiation and proceed with your strategy decisions.

Client's	**Opponent's**
Deal Points ____________	Deal Points ____________
Secondary Points ____________	Secondary Points ____________
Trade Points ____________	Trade Points ____________

§ 4.16 Stay Flexible Because Goals Change

We must issue a word of caution—goals can, and often do, change. Just because you accurately perceive your opponent's objectives today does not necessarily mean his objectives will remain constant over the course of the negotiation. The longer a negotiation is drawn out, the greater the likelihood that one of the parties will change his objectives. This is why one of the most successful tactics used by defense lawyers is delay.

Protracting a negotiation frequently causes adjustment in one of the parties' expectation levels. Even though anyone is susceptible to altering his objectives, completing the goal analysis at the outset will, at the very least, provide you with the parameters of the negotiation. Identifying the goals of all the parties is analogous to drawing the boundaries of an athletic playing field before the game. Knowing where the game will be played is always preferable to looking for the stadium and never finding it.

§ 4.17 Formulating a Strategic Walk-Away Position

One last bit of essential prenegotiation contingency planning will prove to be your insurance policy against disaster. That is devising a strategic walk-away position. In their classic book, *Getting to Yes*, Roger Fisher and William Ury refer to this final phase of preparation as BATNA (Best Alternative to a Negotiated Agreement). It involves identifying all of your viable alternatives to a negotiated agreement.

After doing so, rank them in order of priority from the most attractive to the least attractive. If at any time during the give and take of bargaining, you suddenly find that the negotiation has fallen below the floor you set as the absolute minimum acceptable position as represented by your deal points with no hope of returning, it is time to invoke your BATNA and walk away from the deal.

§ 4.18 The Benefits of BATNA

This process ensures that you will never finish a negotiation in a worse position than when you started. If you accept the premise that, for a negotiation to be successful, any final agreement must result in a net gain over the existing status quo as represented by your deal points, it follows that anything short of obtaining your basic objectives should be a clear signal to abort discussions and walk away from the negotiation.

By identifying your goals as well as your BATNA at the outset, you effectively insulate yourself from having to identify alternatives in a pressurized situation. You also avoid the common trap of substituting your objective goals for the more subjective and less rational alternative of making a deal for the sake of the deal without regard to whether your interests are advanced.

By developing a BATNA or strategic walk-away position before the negotiation begins, you are completely protected from a bad deal. Additionally, when you decide to walk, your BATNA will ensure you walk to your next best available alternative to a negotiated conclusion, whatever that might be.

§ 4.19 The Best BATNA Benefit of All

If the foregoing were not enough, here is the best BATNA benefit of all. Few negotiations, like trials, ever totally go your way. There will be setbacks, surprises, and disappointments. That is guaranteed. When things begin to go bad and pressure mounts, you will have already made the tough decisions. Can the same be said of those sitting across the negotiating table? If they are smart and took the time to prepare, the answer is yes. But human nature being what it is, how many negotiators actually take the time to do it right? This translates into a tremendous advantage for you and your client, provided that you take the time to take preparation seriously.

§ 4.20 Stay Alert to Pre-Packaged Preparation

As a general rule, a lawyer should develop an agenda before starting to negotiate. An agenda can serve as an outline, plan, or merely a checklist for the negotiators as well as a scorecard to help tabulate results and evaluate the final outcome. Take note of what has been omitted from the agenda. Often, topics that are not included are far more revealing than ones that are stated.

Agendas allow negotiators to arrange their issues in a way that is favorable to their position. For instance, some negotiators believe in dealing with the most important issues first. Others prefer to resolve the less important issues at the beginning of a negotiation to establish the momentum that will help carry them through the more difficult issues. Still other negotiators like to link issues together, choosing to resolve problems in combinations rather than dealing with them individually. Regardless of the approach, the objective is the same—to gain the advantage by attempting to control and sequence the topics for discussion.

Rarely in business negotiations will either side present the other with a formal agenda. Custom and practice, especially in the United States, dictate a more informal approach. But that doesn't mean agendas are not at play; they just aren't being revealed. A trip to an auto dealership illustrates the potential dangers of the hidden agenda.

The Hidden Agenda: Lou has just turned 16 and, as promised, his father, Greg, is taking him shopping for his first car. At the dealership, Lou eyes a new Ford Mustang. Sensing Lou's interest, the salesman introduces himself and invites Lou and Greg into his office. Once they're seated, the salesman produces a preprinted order form that contains a checklist of the items to be determined before the sale can be completed.

Of course the salesman never refers to it as an agenda - it's an order form. With the form in front of him, the salesman asks a series of questions. "What color did you have in mind, Lou?" "Did you want the CD player?" "What about a sunroof?" "You want the alloy wheel covers, don't you?" The salesman continues until he has covered all of the items on the order form. At this point in the negotiation, he has not yet brought up price. It is no accident that the salesman's agenda calls for talking about price only after the parties have psychologically committed to a new red Mustang complete with CD player, sunroof, and alloy wheel covers.

Ultimately, when the deal is concluded, Greg will sign off on the preprinted form which contains all the terms the car dealer wants covered. The salesman has scripted the negotiation down to the last penny, while Greg has unwittingly followed the hidden agenda. The lesson is clear: There is always an agenda, hidden or otherwise. Some agendas will be highly specific; others will be vague and ill-defined. Nevertheless, your opposition wouldn't be talking to you in the first place if he didn't want something. Be aware of what that is or forfeit a significant opportunity to the other side. Conversely, be sure to have your own agenda. The more certain you are of your objectives, the more effective you will be in sequencing them with your own bargaining script.

Procedures and Policies: Procedures and policies are similar to agendas. Put simply, they are someone's way of doing something. You should always remember that someone else's procedure or policy isn't necessarily yours. The next time a negotiator uses the "company policy" ploy to win a concession, simply announce your own policy and insist that it control. Once you and your opponent reach an impasse, compromise usually follows.

As with agendas, keep in mind that everything is negotiable, including policies and procedures. Sometimes you'll have the leverage to carry the day; sometimes you won't. But negotiating the point beats conceding as soon as someone says, "That goes against our standard policy." Two can play that game. Make sure you know the rules.

5

Opening Moves: How to Seize Control of the Negotiation

§ 5.01 Introduction

You are a lawyer representing a major media company. The president of the company authorizes you to begin secret negotiations to acquire controlling interest in a primary competitor. You know that if the press learned of the negotiations, the deal would be put in jeopardy. What is your opening move?

Your law firm specializes in insurance defense. You receive word that a $5 million wrongful death suit has been filed against your client's insured stemming from a multi-fatality construction accident. What is your opening move?

A well-known divorce lawyer calls your office and tells you he represents the wife of a wealthy client. The lawyer states that he has very damaging evidence against your client and that he intends to use it unless your client agrees to grant a quick, uncontested divorce and enter into a costly property settlement agreement. What is your opening move?

Every lawyer has his own list of war stories involving worried clients facing every sort of problem imaginable. In all but a handful of cases, negotiation plays the primary role in ultimately resolving the situation. In each instance, the lawyer must sort out the facts, identify the problem, and then make an opening move that will put the negotiation process into motion. Unfortunately, too many lawyers jump into action prematurely without giving sufficient attention to the client's overall objectives and the consequences of their actions. Leaping before looking is common in a busy law practice, especially when the lawyer is being pressured by a panic-stricken client who wants action *now*! While this response to a problem situation is certainly understandable, it often leads to disastrous results. When this occurs, it is the client who suffers and the lawyer who takes the blame.

§ 5.02 Restraint: The First Rule of Opening a Negotiation

Determining exactly when and how to initiate a negotiation can be like driving to an appointment in a hurry, only to be caught by a red light. You fidget impatiently while waiting for what seems like an eternity before the light changes color. As soon as you see green, your impulse is to charge ahead without looking to see if the other cars have honored the traffic signal. The result may be a trip to an auto body shop and sometimes to the hospital. The lesson is clear. Just because the light is green does not necessarily mean you should go. The cautious driver will pause long enough to ascertain whether he can proceed safely. The negotiator should do the same.

Despite the sense of immediacy that is generally associated with representing legal clients, restraint should be the first rule governing all opening move decisions. For example, just because another lawyer phones your office and demands to speak to you about a pending matter does not mean it will be to your advantage to comply with his request. Just because a client is overly anxious to conclude an agreement in the shortest time possible does not mean it is in her best interest to do so. When it comes to making your opening move or responding to someone else's, always be guided by what is in your best interest rather than you're adversary's. If it means waiting a day or two, do it.

On the other hand, if you see an opportunity to expedite a negotiation to your benefit, you should act accordingly. There is certainly no magic in delay merely for the sake of delay. However, pausing to assess the many implications of a specific move or proposal often leads to agreements and settlements based more on reason and less on reaction. This approach is always preferable to paying litigation counsel to deal with problems the negotiation should have resolved. Unfortunately, it is substantially easier to sell this approach to your client after the reality of the litigator's bill for services rendered has had time to register.

§ 5.03 A Common Opening Move Blunder: The Giveaway

A common blunder that illustrates the negotiation axiom "stop, look, and listen" is the giveaway. It usually goes like this: Your client has reached an agreement in principle with another company regarding a business transaction. While the major points have been worked out, numerous issues of varying importance are either still up in the air or have not been addressed at all. Many of these issues are of no real consequence, while others are potentially troublesome. Rather than face up to these thorny issues, the two businesspeople take the easy way out by deciding to "leave the details to the lawyers." In truth, they are leaving out not only details, but also some very controversial points that could prove fatal to the agreement.

A few hours after the agreement in principle has been reached, you receive a call from your client who is bubbling with optimism. He gives you a thumbnail sketch of the deal and tells you to expect a call from the other party's lawyer to work out the details. He concludes the conversation by telling you it is all routine and that he is leaving for a well-earned week to Hawaii to celebrate his latest coup. Ten minutes later, the other lawyer calls. After some obligatory small talk, you get down to business. The opposing lawyer suggests that you resolve as many noncontroversial matters as possible to expedite preparation of the documents. Thinking this makes sense, you agree. He ticks off five or six points that his client would like your client to agree to. To each you respond with a "no problem" or "fine."

Ten minutes into the conversation, he gets around to a zinger that your client probably never thought about but one that you know he should not or would not agree to. Cordiality quickly dissolves into confrontation as the first impasse develops. The conversation ends abruptly as you promise to run it by your client when he returns from Honolulu, knowing all the while that he will never agree to the other lawyer's proposal.

What is wrong with this approach? Simply this: The next time you call the lawyer with requests that you feel are non-controversial, you will most likely find him willing to agree, but only if you will make some concessions of your own. Suddenly, you realize that you have given away most of your trade points without anything to show for it. As a result, you are faced with compromising a previously non-negotiable point or, in the alternative, stonewalling the opposition, thus putting the entire deal at risk. Either option leaves you at a decided disadvantage.

§ 5.04 Do Not Get Caught by the Giveaway

The lawyer in this example could easily have avoided this dilemma by making himself unavailable to negotiate until he had time to review the entire deal with his client and formulate a negotiation plan that would have identified problem areas. Unfortunately, this was not the case, thus allowing the opposing lawyer, who had prepared his negotiating plan, to seize an initial advantage. Fortunately, this does not have to happen to you.

§ 5.05 Common Opening Move Traps to Avoid

The giveaway is only one example of how a premature opening move can detrimentally affect a negotiation. Other common traps associated with failure to consider your opening move carefully include:

- overreaction;
- saying too much;
- failure to verify important information;
- acting on insufficient information;
- failure to grasp points of procedure;

- inadequate preparation;
- revealing strategic plans;
- revealing leverage positions;
- unwittingly tipping off the opposition to your future moves.

PRACTICE TIP: As with the giveaway, most of these pitfalls can be avoided by approaching a negotiation cautiously. A key phrase that will serve you well in constructing the appropriate opening move or response is "Reflect rather than react."

---

§ 5.06 The Five Functions of the Opening Move

Because the "opening move" sets the tone of a negotiation and can often play a crucial role in exerting and maintaining control, it is important to understand fully its functions and limitations. Generally speaking, you should try to only accomplish the following five objectives when making your opening move:

1. Gather information.
2. Build rapport.
3. Balance perceptions.
4. Define negotiation parameters.
5. Make initial use of leverage.

§ 5.07 Gather Information

The opening round of any negotiation can be very useful in gaining information about the opposition that can be evaluated and utilized at a later stage. This function of the opening move is absolutely essential for effective creation and use of leverage. It is also the only way to avoid the traps of miscalculation and taking action based on insufficient or erroneous information.

Initial conversations or exchange of correspondence can often reveal the opposition's negotiating objectives, leverage positions, and internal deadlines. They can also help identify the real decision-makers, disclose points of procedure, and provide insight into the personalities of the opposition. All of these points of information are essential to completing the preparation phase of a given negotiation.

Practice Tip: Beyond these points of essential information, any knowledge gained from the initial stages of the negotiation is potentially valuable. The more extensive your knowledge base, the better position you will be in to deal effectively with the opposition. It is imperative to learn as much as possible before formulating a position that may take the form of a binding offer or a response to an offer. A miscalculation based on insufficient or erroneous information is the stuff of which ulcers and lost clients are made.

Where to find the information you need: There are numerous techniques for using the initial stage of a negotiation to gather information.

The most obvious and often most effective is to ask questions. "What does your client want?" "Who is making the final decision?" "When do you have to know something?" A surprising number of lawyers will simply respond to your questions even when it might not be in their best interest to do so.

The "get acquainted" phone call or lunch: Another technique is the "get acquainted" phone call or lunch. This offers an opportunity to communicate with the other side in a relaxed atmosphere. You will likely pick up valuable bits of information and have a chance to assess the opposing lawyer's personal negotiating style while having to reveal little of your own position or style.

Invite the opposition to make an offer: Other information-gathering techniques include inducing the other side to send a proposed contract draft or letter outlining the terms of an initial offer. Analyzing such documents can help provide information about the other party's positions without the risk of having to reveal your own prematurely.

Utilize standard sources of information: *Martindale-Hubbell* is always a good starting point for gaining insight into your opponent, just as *Dun and Bradstreet* and *Standard & Poor's* are sources of information about various industries and executives that could be relevant to the transaction in question. With the ongoing evolution of the Internet, doing homework on the other side has never been easier.

Check with your client: In many instances, your client will have access to knowledge or information that he may not think will be useful but that in fact could be highly relevant to some aspect of the negotiation. It often comes down to asking the right questions.

Information is the key to success: Regardless of whether a negotiation centers around a business acquisition, personal injury litigation, a collective-bargaining dispute, or any of a thousand and one conceivable topics, information is the key to your ultimate success. It will always be necessary to compile as much information as possible about the subject matter and personalities involved before you will be able to formulate an intelligent negotiation position and plan. We have all heard the horror stories about the attorney who settled a case for less than the claim was worth only because of insufficient or erroneous information. This is why comprehensive information gathering should be a primary objective of your opening move.

§ 5.08 Establish a Rapport with the Opposing Counsel

In the real world of practicing lawyers, the negotiation process is rarely a screaming battlefield of demands, threats, and ultimatums. In the first place, few negotiators possess the overwhelming degree of bargaining strength needed to back up such an approach. Second, and more important, such an approach generally does little except to alienate the other party into finding an alternative to dealing with heavy-handed lawyers and clients. This is not to say that the hardball approach does not exist or should not be used in certain circumstances; however, in the great majority of cases it is simply inappropriate and not effective.

Contrary to the way they may be depicted in fiction, most negotiations are based, at least to some degree, on a cooperative process where the emphasis is on compromise and problem solving. A good, working rapport with the opposing party is absolutely essential if this approach is to succeed. Establishing this rapport is another important function of the opening move.

Don't confuse rapport with weakness: We caution you not to confuse rapport with behavior that could be perceived as a signal of weakness or uncertainty. The correct approach is to project a sense of natural ease and openness, balanced by self-confidence, efficiency, and firmness.

The problem of too much rapport: While a good rapport with the other lawyer is usually desirable, it can be a stumbling block when rapport turns into overfamiliarity. This is a real problem in smaller communities and within certain concentrated industries where lawyers find themselves repeatedly negotiating with the same people. To make matters worse, they often encounter their negotiating counterparts just as frequently on the golf course or in professional and community activities. In these instances, rapport is often already established, or in some cases has gone beyond the realm of possibility due to past battles not forgotten.

If you find yourself in such a position, be on guard to avoid unconscious patterns that make you predictable, and resist the tendency to let personal feelings influence professional judgments. This is a very real problem in many sectors of practice. It can produce subtle, yet substantial negative repercussions at the bargaining table. Awareness is the only way to avoid this insidious enemy against your effectiveness.

To illustrate the problem, consider the unfortunate case of Mr. Fore. Mr. Fore is a plaintiff's lawyer practicing in a medium-size Midwestern city. In the past, his only problem was predictability. Fore's standard operating procedure in personal injury cases was to demand approximately three times the amount for which he was willing to settle his case. The insurance defense bar privately nicknamed him "Three Times Fore" because they knew his bottom-line assessment of the case's worth as soon as he made his initial demand. Unfortunately for Mr. Fore, it took several years for him to realize what his opposition had already figured out. Fortunately for Mr. Fore, he was able to correct this habit, but not before it cost him and his clients a substantial amount of money in lost settlements over the years.

PRACTICE TIP: The problem of constantly negotiating with the same faces poses numerous opportunities to lose effectiveness at the bargaining table. Speaking too freely, failing to move aggressively, or letting down your guard with familiar adversaries are all realities facing any practicing lawyer. It takes constant effort to combat this subtle and often unconscious form of negotiating ineffectiveness.

---

§ 5.09 Balance Perceptions to Build Your Credibility

When we speak of rapport with opposing counsel, we are not just referring to personal pleasantry. Building credibility and respect in the eyes of the opposing lawyer is critical to conducting an effective negotiation. Ideally, all lawyers and clients engaged in negotiation would be of equal age and reputation with each possessing the same relative degree of experience, ability, resources, and bargaining strength. We all know this is seldom the case. There will always be disparities, both real and perceived. The opening move is the time to balance these disparate perceptions. Failure to at least neutralize or partially offset negative perceptions at the outset will most likely result in a disjointed, defensive posture for the rest of the negotiation.

The young lawyer versus the old pro: Take the example of a young lawyer who is pitted against a veteran practition. The natural perception of the older lawyer is that his counterpart is inexperienced, uncertain, and thus at a competitive disadvantage. On the other hand, the younger lawyer will often assume that the older lawyer is more knowledgeable and generally more competent to represent his client. Of course, these common assumptions are not always true; however, perceptions are what count. For this reason, the younger lawyer must use the opening move to balance these disparities or perceived disparities.

The correct initial approach by the younger lawyer is to be more reserved and formal than he might be with a lawyer his own age. His tone and substance should convey an image of self-confidence, firmness, and complete familiarity with the facts and law involved in the matter being discussed. He must also take every opportunity to convey subtly to his older opponent that his initial impressions were inaccurate. While, in many cases, this sense of calm, cool assuredness may be an act, it is essential that it be a convincing one to balance the perceptions held by the more experienced lawyer.

Prizefights and negotiations: The opening rounds of a negotiation are much like a prizefight. Each lawyer is probing for weaknesses that can be exploited later. Awareness of this process is essential in order to convey the right signals. If the opponent does not respect or trust you in the early stages of bargaining, you are in for some rough going in the later rounds. If your opponent spots a weakness early, she is sure to exploit it later. If you give your opponent an opening, she is likely to go for a knockout punch. It is your job to prevent any of this from happening while sizing up the opposition for yourself.

Practice Tip: Building a rapport, establishing respect and trust, and balancing negative perceptions should all be interwoven into your opening move. The key to achieving success in all of these areas is an ongoing awareness that, while you should be probing the opposition, also know that the opposition is doing the same thing to you. This awareness should be followed with projecting the right signals to your opponent. These signals will, of course, vary with the circumstances, personalities, and subject matter. Awareness and flexibility provide the "one-two" combination to get things off on the right foot.

---

§ 5.10 Define Your Negotiation Parameters

An important function of any opening move is to define the parameters of a particular negotiation. This simply means identifying the issues and objectives considered important by the opposition as well as the outside limits or settlement range relating to those issues. Of course, you will want to do as much of this as possible in the preparation phase; however, it is virtually impossible to appreciate the other side's position fully until you reach the opening move stage.

§ 5.11 How to Set Up the Floor/Ceiling Trap

The oldest method of identifying negotiating parameters is inviting the other side to make an offer. This has the effect of creating either a ceiling or a floor to the negotiation. For instance, suppose the lawyer for the buyer invites his counterpart to disclose what the seller would be willing to accept. A low initial offer ($4.5 million) by the seller effectively establishes a ceiling. This tells the buyer that the maximum he would have to pay is less than the stated price. This offer would also lead most people to believe that the ultimate purchase price could be lowered through more negotiation.

On the other hand, a high initial offer ($7 million) could be viewed as simply being beyond reality. In light of time constraints, the buyer might feel it would be fruitless to pursue further negotiations and might begin to seek an alternative acquisition immediately.

In both examples, the party making the offer is at a disadvantage.

Two ways to escape the floor/ceiling trap: There are two solutions to this common dilemma. The first is to decline making an offer and to invite the other side to make the first move. Sometimes this works. However, most times a game of "first offer ping-pong" ensues.

Talk in ranges rather than specifics: The other approach is to talk in terms of ranges. The seller's response would be something like this:

"Well, we feel the company is probably worth in the neighborhood of $4.5 to $6 million." While this establishes a ceiling, it is a flexible one with plenty of room for give and take. Generally, this type of offer will elicit a response ranging from anger to disbelief ("I'm shocked!") to concurrence ("Well, that's probably a little high, but it's in the ballpark.").

Practice Tip: Revealing parameters is potentially dangerous. There will be some negotiations where candor may be the best policy. The only guideline we offer is to assess your situation very carefully before choosing this approach.

You do not have to be held prisoner by your mistakes: In the event you unwittingly fall into the floor/ceiling trap or tip off the other side as to time pressures, remember that this does not have to spell disaster. Negotiation has no rules except the ones you make or accept. Just because you make a low initial offer does not mean you have to be bound by it. The same is true of deadlines. Whenever practical, retract your offer and come in higher or find an alternate way to deal with your time pressures. While the circumstances will not always allow this, do it whenever possible. If you cannot retract your offer and the consequences of a deal would be counterproductive, remember that your ultimate option is to walk away from the deal. You are always better off with no deal than with a bad deal.

§ 5.12 Initial Use of Leverage

The last function of the opening move is the initial use of leverage. To illustrate, assume that a prospective buyer of a widget factory knew the approximate price range that the seller would accept. Also assume that the seller was eager for a quick cash deal. Based on this information, the buyer's lawyer could invoke the leverage of timing and uncertainty by offering to buy the company for $4.5 million with 10 percent down and the balance financed with a 10-year payout. Alternatively, he could offer $3.75 million in cash with a 15-day closing as a condition precedent to the deal. In either event, the buyer would accomplish its objectives.

If the seller chose the first option, the buyer would purchase the company for $500,000 less than it was willing to pay and would still have plenty of time to locate an alternative acquisition. If the seller selected option number two, which is much more likely under the circumstances, the buyer would be able to buy the company at a bargain price while also building in a time cushion to find an alternate acquisition should the seller have second thoughts.

Conversely, if the seller was privy to the buyer's internal deadline, he should convey strong interest in the deal without settling on a specific price. Subtle delay tactics calculated on extending the negotiation beyond the point where it would be realistic for the buyer to seek an alternative acquisition would accompany this strategy. Once this point was reached, the seller could count on receiving a higher purchase price, provided it is within the predetermined $5 million maximum figure the buyer authorized.

This is only one illustration of how the opening move can be used to exert leverage. The variations are as numerous as the different fact situations that confront you and will largely be determined by how extensive your knowledge base is.

§ 5.13 A Word of Caution

Remember that the opening move tactics you use will surely be used against you. This is why any signal from the opposition should be analyzed and investigated as thoroughly as possible before a response is made. To this end, we reemphasize, "Reflect rather than react."

§ 5.14 How to Make the Opening Move

Almost every negotiation involving nonlawyers is initiated by one of four means: direct personal contact, telephone, correspondence, or e-mail. Lawyers are uniquely endowed with a fifth means, the lawsuit. There is certainly no hard-and-fast rule as to which avenue is most effective. This will depend on the particular circumstances and personalities of the parties as well as the goals of the client and the negotiating styles of the parties. Each approach has its advantages and disadvantages.

§ 5.15 How to Handle Direct Personal Contact

The meeting, like computers and expense accounts, is a staple in the world of business and law. Whether the site is an office, restaurant, or golf course, this is often the best way to get the ball rolling, especially in a business setting. It usually starts with one lawyer making an offhand comment or overture to another lawyer or business executive that he has a client interested in establishing a business relationship, provided terms and conditions could be worked out to everyone's satisfaction. The primary benefit of the direct approach is immediacy. In addition to establishing that the other party might be interested in the proposed deal, there is the opportunity for feedback and elaboration as well as the chance to observe the other person's reaction and demeanor. For this reason, the information function can be maximized through the personal meeting.

§ 5.16 The Downside of Personal Contact

The downside of the personal contact approach is the tendency to disclose too much or make ill-advised statements without time for investigation or reflection. This is especially true for the person to whom the proposal is being made. These potential dangers tend to be magnified in more relaxed settings such as over lunch or at a cocktail party. The best out is to "take it under advisement" and change the subject if you feel as if you are drifting into dangerous waters.

Beyond proposing a "deal," in a business setting, the personal approach is probably not the best vehicle for initiating a negotiation aimed at resolving conflict. This is especially true if the subject matter deals with controversial or potentially troubling issues or if litigation is a possible alternative to agreement.

§ 5.17 How to Handle an Opening Move by Telephone

The telephone serves much the same function as the person-to-person approach, with several notable exceptions.

§ 5.18 Control

The person calling is always able to control the initial subject matter and timing of the contact. Additionally, the caller enjoys an edge in preparation. Conversely, the person being called often falls victim to surprise and is rarely prepared to the same extent as the caller.

The best way to counter the surprise element is simply to choose not to take the call. You can simply be "in a meeting," "in court," "busy," or "unavailable." Experienced legal secretaries have a marvelous facility for handling these situations with the utmost tact and cordiality. The rule governing use of the telephone to initiate a negotiation or to respond to an overture is to do it only when you consider it an opportunity. The giveaway is a clear example of how a lawyer was able to use the telephone to seize control of a negotiation to the detriment of someone totally unprepared to negotiate.

§ 5.19 Benefits of the Telephone

As with the meeting, the telephone can be an effective instrument when it comes to commencing a business-related negotiation. Because facial reactions can be concealed while allowing for immediate feedback, the telephone can sometimes prove effective in disputes involving potential litigation. A call to another lawyer can often help define issues, provide background information, and establish a rapport without going into the substantive aspects related to the problem at hand. As with the potential downside risks inherent in the face-to-face meeting, preparation and self-control are essential so as not to disclose information prematurely or add to the level of hostility stemming from the dispute. Beyond these basic objectives, you are probably best advised to avoid the telephone until you have sufficient information to formulate a position.

§ 5.20 Additional Points for Handling Telephone Negotiations

When the telephone is used, keep the following points in mind.

Take notes: Detailed note taking provides a record of the conversation. Commitments, concessions, and points of information can often get lost over the course of a protracted negotiation. A dated phone memorandum form in the file can be a potentially powerful leverage device, especially if the opposition attempts to modify earlier positions and understandings reached over the phone.

Use a telephone agenda list: How many times have you completed a telephone conversation only to realize that an important point was never discussed? A checklist of items to be discussed is a must before using the telephone to negotiate. This is the only effective way to ensure the call will be focused on the subject matter you want discussed.

Calculators, pens, and paper: These are three essentials that should always be close to your telephone. These items keep you organized and help you make or understand calculations that may be necessary to the conversation.

Resist pressure to respond: Because of the immediacy of the telephone, there is often pressure to respond to questions, positions, or offers. The dangers inherent in this type of behavior have already been discussed. Self-control is the only way to offset this human tendency. Remember, there is no rule that says you have to respond to anything. Often, the best approach is to say as little as possible or nothing at all.

§ 5.21 How to Use Correspondence Effectively in the Opening Move

Correspondence plays an important role in all phases of negotiation. Its many uses and functions will be analyzed in succeeding chapters dealing with maintaining control, fallback techniques, and closing, as well as in a chapter devoted solely to correspondence. From the standpoint of the opening move, correspondence is most commonly used by lawyers in situations involving contested claims and potential litigation. The role of correspondence in business-related negotiations is generally reserved for later stages once the negotiation has been initiated. The primary exception to this is the "Dear John" business letter used to decline to pursue a proposed deal.

§ 5.22 The Demand Letter

The demand letter is the vehicle most lawyers use to initiate lawsuit settlement negotiations. The demand letter serves several functions. First, it provides notice of a claim and advises the adversary that the claimant is being represented by a lawyer. From a more subtle standpoint, the demand letter sets the tone for the negotiation.

A well-drafted, detailed letter helps substantiate the plaintiff's demand while also communicating the lawyer's style, which helps build her credibility. A well-thought-out, carefully drafted letter summarizing the facts on which a case rests and concluding with a demand of varying specificity will be given much more serious consideration than a two-paragraph, bare-bones notice of representation followed by an exorbitant demand. The latter type of demand letter will most likely be ignored or treated by the opposition with varying degrees of hostility or amusement. Demand letters are discussed in detail in Chapter 8, which deals with correspondence.

§ 5.23 E-mail

E-mail is not generally the medium of choice for initiating a negotiation. We would never recommend using e-mail until a relationship has been established. But that does not mean that your adversary might not use e-mail in an attempt to open a negotiation. Our advice is to refrain from such overtures and to insist on one of the more traditional methods already discussed. Once you feel comfortable with the situation and with the other lawyer, by all means use e-mail if it fits into your plan. But remember, when it comes to delay, it is much more difficult to dodge e-mail messages, especially if you have previously used the medium and now have had a change of heart. The same advice applies to traditional correspondence sent by fax.

§ 5.24 Filing Suit

As with anything else, there are downside risks associated with filing suit as your opening move. First and most important, if you represent a plaintiff, always remember the familiar axiom that the best defense is a good offense. You can rest assured that the defendant's lawyer will do his best to conjure up a counterclaim that invariably will carry a prayer for relief in excess of yours. Even if there is no counterclaim, there is no guarantee that the defendant will respond with anything more than a general denial. Credibility and burden of proof are two primary factors that will determine how eager the defense is to enter into any negotiations beyond disposing of the nuisance value of the suit.

> ***PRACTICE TIP:*** It is best to file lawsuits only after carefully considering the implications. Using an ill-advised lawsuit to bluff the opposition into a settlement is a calling card for disaster. On the other hand, if your client has a strong claim, you will enhance your chances for a negotiated settlement by using the suit as leverage.

§ 5.25 Success Is Ultimately Up to You

Regardless of the method you use to initiate a negotiation, your chances for success will depend largely on the circumstances of the case, your level of preparation, and, most important, your skill in executing the opening move. Knowing what to do certainly helps in this regard, but in the final analysis your level of success will be determined by your own legal and interpersonal skills. This is why there is simply no substitute for rolling up your sleeves and doing it right.

Your personal skills combined with the opening move principles set forth in this chapter provide you with an irresistible combination that will allow you to seize control of more than your share of negotiations. While this does not guarantee an ideal result every time out, it sure beats the alternatives.

6 Maintaining Control at Every Stage of the Negotiation

§ 6.01 Introduction

A primary objective of the opening move is to gain control of the negotiation. Once this is accomplished, the emphasis should shift to maintaining control at every stage of the bargaining process. Control, like anything else worthwhile, does not just happen. It is the product of calculated, assertive actions designed to achieve predetermined objectives. This entails recognizing the type and degree of control needed for a given situation, followed by positive steps designed to realize your control objective.

When you fail to assert yourself, you often will find yourself being controlled. The common and seemingly automatic process of airline seat selection best illustrates this principle. Most people who fly regularly have certain preferences regarding where they want to sit. If you do not like to be cramped and like to look at the scenery, your requirements are fairly clear. Yet, how many times have you presented your ticket to the agent only to wind up feeling like a flying sardine wedged into the middle seat between a professional wrestler and a linebacker for the Dallas Cowboys. In the days when smoking was allowed on domestic flights, it was much worse. You were liable to be stuffed in the middle seat while inhaling everybody else's secondhand smoke.

This unfortunate situation could have been avoided simply by informing the agent that you wanted a window seat where you could spread out, preferably on the emergency exit row where there is extra legroom. By not doing so, you relinquished control over an important aspect of a flight that was already costing you hundreds of dollars. For that kind of money, it is not unreasonable to want to be comfortable. To make matters worse, the agent most likely would have honored your request had you only spoken up.

§ 6.02 Asserting Yourself Is a Key to Controlling a Negotiation

Speaking up is a key to asserting control over a negotiation. If your opponent suggests a meeting at an inconvenient time, simply tell her you are tied up. If you are trying to establish a place to negotiate, do not hesitate to suggest your preference rather than automatically responding with a "you name it" or "anywhere is fine with me." By failing to speak up, you fail to seize opportunities to exert control over various elements of the negotiation.

This is not to suggest that controlling a negotiation is always as simple as just expressing your preference, though it often can be. There will be times when it will be inappropriate, unfeasible, or simply impossible to assert the type or degree of control you would like. However, having an awareness of what you want to accomplish followed by taking steps to achieve your objectives will generally make a marked difference when it comes to totaling up the bottom line. Because control plays such an important role in your ultimate success, it is valuable to focus on specific control techniques that can be used in every negotiation situation you might encounter.

§ 6.03 Choosing the Time and Place to Negotiate

You can gain an immediate advantage over your opponent by controlling when and where a negotiation will be conducted. Definite tactical and psychological advantages flow to the negotiator capable of controlling these seemingly insignificant factors. Surprisingly, many lawyers allow their opponents to gain the upper hand by surrendering control of these tactical aspects of bargaining. Forfeiting an opportunity to exert control over time and place is often the first step to letting the process control you. Fortunately, this is a mistake that can often be avoided by simply taking the initiative to suggest a time and place to negotiate, or, conversely, by not automatically agreeing to any proposal the opposing lawyer may suggest.

§ 6.04 My Office or Yours?

Most negotiators perform their work with greater confidence and efficiency in a familiar setting. Consequently, you are apt to be more relaxed and mentally sharper if you are able to conduct a negotiation in your own office or other comfortable and familiar surroundings. In addition to comfort and familiarity, the negotiator with the home-office advantage has complete control over the temperature, lighting, seating arrangement, scheduled breaks, use of assistants, and presence or absence of interruptions. On the other hand, the visitor is subjected to an array of unfamiliar circumstances that makes it more difficult to perform at optimum levels.

This edge is analogous to the home-court advantage in college basketball. It has been documented that home-court advantage is a tangible factor that translates into victories even when the home team squares off against teams with superior talent.

Within the context of a law practice, the value of the home-office advantage is well illustrated by an emotion-charged property settlement and custody negotiation incident to a divorce. The very nature of any contested domestic matter is cause for a great deal of tension and anxiety. A lawyer can raise the anxiety level by scheduling the opposing party's deposition at his office. The fear of the unknown coupled with an unfamiliar setting will likely cause the deposed party to experience extreme anxiety as the deposition date nears. This heightened anxiety may result in the opponent's granting concessions or agreeing to less desirable settlement terms just to avoid the unpleasant confrontation. Additionally, the added edge of a familiar environment can help you and your client deal with the situation from a position of strength and security in contrast to the uncertainty and anxiety the opposition is experiencing.

§ 6.05 One Instance When Your Opponent's Office Is Preferable

If you have decided to employ anger coupled with a walkout tactic, consider negotiating at your opponent's office. It is easier to play out this move in your opponent's office rather than your own. While this tactic is rarely employed, it can prove useful in extreme situations.

§ 6.06 Home Away from Home

If you are unable to persuade your opponent to negotiate at your office, attempt to schedule another location favorable to you. For example, if your opponent is reluctant to come to your office to negotiate, invite her to lunch at your business club where you will still feel at home. If you are still unsuccessful, invite your opponent to lunch at a restaurant that is mutually agreeable or to a business club where both of you are members. The key is to maintain your comfort and familiarity level whenever possible.

§ 6.07 How to Offset Your Opponent's Home-Office Advantage

Always try to avoid your opponent's office unless you have a tactical reason for going there or unless you simply have no choice. When you are forced to negotiate at your opponent's office, you should take steps to offset this advantage. Visiting your opponent's office to discuss less important issues can do this. After one or two visits, you will have acquired a feel for the surroundings, thereby reducing your opponent's advantage when crucial aspects of the negotiation will be decided.

Practice Tip: Whenever it is necessary for your client to accompany you into unfamiliar territory, try to remove as much uncertainty as possible by describing what the client will encounter and what will probably happen. Your client will not only appreciate your efforts, but will perform much better. Remember, for many clients, a visit to your office is difficult enough; a trip to the opposing lawyer's office can be an ordeal.

§ 6.08 Taking Your Cue to Assert Control

Too many negotiators fail to realize the importance of seizing the initiative in a negotiation. The opposing lawyer may ask:

"Does it make any difference to you where we meet?"

"Where do you want to take her deposition?"

"My office or yours?"

"We need to discuss this matter—what about meeting at my office?"

You should instinctively take your cue to seize the opportunity he has created. Even if the actual advantage gained is negligible, making a habit of speaking up helps develop the assertiveness necessary to take charge of other aspects of the negotiation process consistently.

§ 6.09 How About 8:00 Monday Morning?

How do you normally feel at 8:00 Monday morning? If you are like most people, probably not so great. Then why would anyone agree to negotiate at this time, or for that matter any time when he is not capable of functioning at maximum efficiency? Ironically, many lawyers spend countless hours preparing for a negotiation, only to give the other side the advantage by routinely agreeing to meet at inconvenient times.

§ 6.10 Controlling Internal and External Schedules

People have certain times of day when they are at their peak. For some, the morning hours are the most productive. Others are at their best in the afternoon, while some prefer evening hours. Alternatively, individuals have some time during every day or week when they do not operate at peak efficiency. Generally, Monday mornings and Friday afternoons are not the most productive times of a workweek. The same can be said of the hour before lunch and closing time. In addition, everyone finds his schedule bottlenecked at various times, which in turn makes completing ordinary tasks more difficult. Using your peak time for important negotiations is another way to assert control over a negotiation. Surprisingly, in the vast majority of situations, your choice of date and time for a negotiation will be accepted without any argument from your opponent. By taking the initiative, you will find that most meetings, telephone conversations, and depositions can be scheduled to suit your time frame.

PRACTICE TIP: A key factor in control is awareness. Be aware of what time of the day and week is right for you, then suggest it to your opponent as a matter of course. When your opponent does the same, do not throw away a potential advantage by indifferently agreeing to a suggestion that would not prove beneficial.

---

§ 6.11 Seizing Unscheduled Opportunities

Sometimes, unscheduled opportunities to negotiate may occur at places and times that would not normally be advantageous for you. If the advantage of the moment outweighs the disadvantages, seize the opportunity. For example, assume you just spent the entire day working on a pending case in anticipation of contacting your opponent the next day to discuss settlement approaches. By the end of the workday, you are quite knowledgeable about the case and have formulated your negotiation strategy. Pleased with your efforts, you stop off at the health club for a workout that leaves you feeling energetic and relaxed.

As you are leaving the locker room, you meet the lawyer whom you intend to contact the next day. It is apparent from his opening remarks that he would like to discuss the case right now. Should you? If you believe the advantages of the moment outweigh the traditional disadvantages, by all means proceed to negotiate. In this example, the advantages of a receptive opponent coupled with being well prepared, mentally and physically alert, and in a relaxed atmosphere far outweigh not being able to discuss the case in your office or at your prime time.

Practice Tip: Be flexible. Opportunity often presents itself when you least expect it. If you are in a position to seize an opportunity, do so. If you are not, chances are that the opportunity is one for your opponent rather than for yourself. If this is the case, avoid the issue until the time is right.

---

§ 6.12 The Importance of Pacing Negotiations

The tempo of any negotiation can be regulated through the use of three control ploys:

- Deadlock
- Delay
- Acceleration

One of these three pacing techniques should fit any situation that may confront you. For instance, certain advantages result from a rapid or fast-paced negotiating tempo. In this situation, you would want to use acceleration tactics to speed up the bargaining process. Conversely, there are distinct advantages to using delay or deadlock tactics. Regardless of the tempo that is appropriate for your particular circumstances and objectives, one of these tactical approaches will enable you to assert some degree of control over the tempo of the negotiation. This enables you to coordinate the right moves with the proper timing.

Unquestionably, smartly executed moves get results. However, the combination of the right move made at the right time can have a synergistic effect in terms of gaining the upper hand over the opposition. The pacing techniques discussed in this section will help you regulate the tempo of a negotiation so that you can derive maximum benefits from each move you make.

§ 6.13 Deadlock—The Rush-Hour Ploy

Have you ever been caught in rush-hour traffic in a large city? As you know, it can be a most frustrating experience. There is something about those endless lines of vehicles creeping toward their destination that seems to frustrate everyone. As you become aggravated and irritated by the traffic jam, emotions run high and tempers flare. As bad as this situation seems, it can get much worse by adding one variable—a deadline.

Imagine the same traffic jam scene on a Friday afternoon as you attempt to reach the airport to catch your flight back home after a long business trip. Your frustration level is at its peak as you impatiently wait for the traffic to start moving. The additional pressure brought on by the deadline has a multiplier effect on your frustration level. Frustration mounts with each passing moment. Your anger is slowly replaced by a feeling of helplessness. This is exactly the effect deadlock has on most negotiators.

Negotiators fear deadlock because of the negative overtones associated with it. Deadlock is synonymous with no agreement. To most negotiators, failure to agree means that objectives have not been met and goals will be unrealized; consequently, the negotiators have failed. Unfortunately, negotiators who have this misconception about deadlock have thrown away one of the most powerful negotiating weapons.

The use of deadlock can bring the entire negotiating process to a halt. It is a sure way to create the ultimate traffic jam in a negotiation. If your goal is to stop the bargaining process in midstream, deadlock will do the job. As a general rule, when maintaining the status quo will not damage your position, deadlock can be used to stop the negotiating process so that the passage of time may uncover or create a weakness in your opposition.

§ 6.14 How to Use Deadlock in the No-Action Situation

Charles Williamson is a three-year veteran of the National Football League. As a relatively low draft selection, he had to overcome a great deal of competition to earn a slot on the team in his rookie year. His dedication and determination enabled him to beat the cut and make the final team roster just prior to the regular season. Charles entered into a three-year contract with the team at the NFL base salary of $285,000 per year in addition to the standard fringe benefits and other compensation incentives. Charles is now in his final year of the three-year contract, and he is eagerly awaiting negotiation of a new contract. Fortunately for Charles, he has been a solid performer for the team and is well liked by the coaching staff and other team members. The general manager of the team lets Charles know that he is willing to discuss contract terms anytime Charles is ready. Charles is fully aware that his marginal position during his rookie year affected his salary. As expected, Charles is eager to negotiate a better deal.

The general manager begins talking to Charles during summer camp about the new contract. The discussions are cordial and candid. The general manager is quick to agree with Charles that a salary increase is in order; however, neither side offers definite figures. The general manager is successful in disposing of all the less controversial, secondary points that Charles agrees are minor in importance. Just prior to the start of the regular season, the parties get to the heart of the contract. Charles finally reveals his salary demands. Not surprisingly, the general manager expresses shock at such a demand. After the initial demand and counteroffer, it appears that Charles and the general manager are still $500,000 per year apart.

At this point, the general manager could attempt to close the gap between Charles's demands and the team's offer by further talks. But, since all the new contract points have been resolved except for salary terms, and since Charles will have to play out the current season under his old contract, the general manager is content with the status quo and decides to use deadlock as a ploy to close the salary gap.

The general manager tells Charles, "I'm prepared to raise my last offer substantially, but that is as high as I can go. Charles, I'm sorry I can't do better, but with rising costs this is the best the team can do. After all, it's much, much better than what you are being paid now. In fact, I will even make the new contract effective immediately so you can earn more money starting with this Sunday's game. Please give it serious consideration—it's my final offer."

The general manager has put the burden to act squarely on Charles. Under the terms of the new offer, each week Charles delays in making a decision he loses money and the general manager saves money, or so it seems. Now Charles is faced with either substantially reducing his demands in order to get closer to what appears to be the team's final offer, or accepting the risks associated with becoming a free agent at the end of the season.

On the other hand, the general manager has chosen deadlock hoping that the passage of time might afford him a negotiating advantage. For instance, should Charles become injured during the season, his future value might be impaired. The same is true if Charles doesn't perform well during the season, or if a high-profile college player becomes a prospect for Charles's position. Any of these events would diminish the value of Charles's service to the team. If Charles has an outstanding year, the general manager could always capitulate and pay the demanded salary. However, chances are that three out of four of the previously mentioned future contingencies will go against Charles, thus diminishing his bargaining strength. As a result, the general manager is content to accept deadlock, for the time being.

§ 6.15 Delay: Making Time Your Ally

Although delay tactics are much more subtle than deadlock ploys, their objective is the same—to control the tempo of the negotiation to gain an advantage. Generally, delay tactics should be used when the passage of time will weaken your opponent's position or improve yours. For example, if your client has just been sued and has instructed you to settle prior to trial, when should you make the initial settlement offer? Although the offer could be made immediately after receiving notice of the lawsuit, this might be viewed as a sign of weakness by the opposition. Delaying your settlement offer until a responsive pleading has been filed will put you in a more advantageous bargaining position.

PRACTICE TIP: Your negotiation posture can be strengthened if a counterclaim is filed as part of your response. This represents a combination of defensive delay and offensive leverage.

---

§ 6.16 Do Not Confuse Delay with Procrastination

Delay should not be confused with procrastination. In the negotiator's world, delay is used as a calculated tactical device to gain a specified advantage over the opposition. Procrastination is neither planned nor calculated. It is a habit of postponing doing something until a future time because of laziness or indifference. In some situations, it may appear that an opponent is procrastinating, when in fact he is using a well-camouflaged delay tactic.

§ 6.17 Buying Time Through Delay

If your opponent is eager to move forward, delay is a good way to slow the tempo, thus allowing you to find out why your opponent is in such a hurry. Generally, the other side will have a reason for stepping up the pace of bargaining. It is usually advisable to find out why. Delay tactics can buy the time needed to do this.

Most lawyers are experts at using delay tactics. This is partially a byproduct of our complex and overworked legal system, which is quite susceptible to delay. Procedural delay can often be used to your clients' advantage. Consider the client who has been sued on an open account. He readily admits that he owes the plaintiff money, but he needs time to raise the money. By filing suit, the plaintiff has in effect given the defendant time to come up with the money by placing the case in the legal pipeline. The process takes time, and time is exactly what the defendant wants. Ultimately, in this case, the defendant will pay the plaintiff what he owes, but not before he is unwittingly granted extra time by the plaintiff's lawsuit.

§ 6.18 Using Acceleration to Bring Matters to a Conclusion

Acceleration is the opposite of deadlock. This control tactic is used when the negotiator wants to speed up the process to take advantage of favorable circumstances.

Acceleration is an action-oriented tactic that can be used by the plaintiff as well as the defendant. Frequently, lawyers who prefer an aggressive negotiating style use acceleration ploys. These lawyers like to keep the pressure on and bring matters to a head. Acceleration tactics are well suited to this style of negotiation.

One example of acceleration is the lawyer who is quick to file suit without issuing any advance warning. Her main objective seems to be getting the case to trial as quickly as possible. Each stage of the negotiation is accelerated to the next, with the ultimate objective being the trial. The objective of acceleration is the same as deadlock and delay—to control the negotiation.

Often acceleration is used to change the status quo. For instance, in a paternity dispute where the mother of the child has been unsuccessful after numerous attempts to persuade the putative father to help support the child, the mother's lawyer may decide it best to depart from the standard practice of issuing a demand letter to the potential defendant. Indeed, the mother's lawyer may decide to accelerate the process by filing suit immediately. Refusing to discuss settlement terms until the discovery phase of the litigation is completed could further accelerate matters. In an extreme situation, acceleration can be taken to the limit by refusing to discuss settlement terms until the day of trial.

Practice Tip: Acceleration spurs action. It is a useful tactic for maintaining control because it forces your opponent to respond to your moves. This forces the opposition into a defensive posture. The result is control of the negotiation.

§ 6.19 How to Use Balancing as a Control Device

The negotiator makes continuing efforts to maintain a favorable bargaining posture, or, at the very least, to preserve a position of equilibrium. As long as the balance of power can be maintained, a negotiator can work from a relatively secure position. However, if the balance of power shifts in favor of one negotiator, the other is forced to deal from a position of weakness. Until the balance of power is restored, each move the disadvantaged negotiator makes takes on the appearance of a rear guard action—certainly not the position of strength.

The need for balancing is ongoing. Concessions gained during the early rounds of a negotiation can be completely or partially lost or their value severely diluted if you are forced to deal from a position of weakness for too long. Consequently, the need to maintain the balance of power with your opposition in order to preserve control is always present at every stage of the negotiation.

§ 6.20 The Two Rules of Balancing

Balancing embraces two simple rules: (1) Do not let your opponent gain the upper hand at any stage of a negotiation, and (2) If your opponent gains the upper hand, move quickly to bring the balance of power into a state of equilibrium.

For instance, if an opponent offers some startling new facts or a surprise witness during settlement negotiations, control may be temporarily lost. Before you make any settlement proposal, you should regain, or at least balance, control. This can be done by coming forward with some new information, facts, witnesses, or law of your own. Meeting threats with counterthreats or answering uncertainty with more uncertainty are additional examples of balancing.

Control is rarely lost by a single dramatic move by the opposition. In the usual case, control ebbs away slowly. Failure to offset a shift in momentum can establish an irreversible trend in favor of the other side. Taking steps to recapture balance as the negotiation unfolds is the best way to maintain the necessary degree of control in the bargaining process.

§ 6.21 Personal Injury Negotiation: The Classic Example of Balancing

Personal injury cases are often classic examples of balancing in action. Consider the usual chain of events in a personal injury case. Someone is injured due to the negligence of another. The negligent party is covered by liability insurance. Consequently, the insurance company has exclusive control over settlement of the injured person's claim during the early stages of the negotiation.

Once the injured person passes through the life-threatening or acute pain phases, concern about receiving payment from the negligent party emerges. Frequently, this concern for compensation is motivated either by revenge or by some idea that the plaintiff will reap a windfall. In these types of cases, the injured party develops a very high expectation level regarding the potential settlement value of the claim. That expectation level is often based on emotional considerations, unrealistic perceptions, or just good old-fashioned misinformation that bears little or no relevance to the actual liability or damages involved.

If the injured person attempts to negotiate with the insurance company at this stage, settlement talks usually tend to break down because of positions adopted by the parties. At this stage, the insurance company has control over the negotiation. Why? Because it is in the business of disposing of claims; consequently, it enjoys a superior knowledge base. The insurance company has a good feel for what an inexperienced claimant, not represented by counsel, is likely to do or not do.

In this example, the insurance company is aware of the injured party's unrealistic demands and is content to hold its position by making an extremely low counteroffer. At this point in the negotiation, the claimant has gained nothing from the insurance company but sympathy and a take-it-or-leave-it settlement offer that is well below the claimant's expectation level. Many unskilled negotiators who try to settle claims without a lawyer would most likely view such a position as hopeless and agree to accept whatever amount the insurance company offers. Consequently, the negotiation ends.

In this scenario, the injured party never had control. Therefore, the claimant's settlement demand never had enough impact to influence the bargaining to a higher level. The result: a poor settlement for the claimant.

§ 6.22 Tilting the Balance of Power

Assume the injured person engages the services of a lawyer. The lawyer explains the law controlling negligence actions, outlines the settlement process, explains such concepts as jury verdict expectancy and the time value of money, and describes the settlement propensities of the subject insurance company. The injured party is now in a much better position to evaluate the strengths and weaknesses of the case. Based on this information, a realistic expectation level and reasonable settlement range for negotiation purposes can be adopted.

By engaging a lawyer, the injured party is able to bring the balance of power back into a state of equilibrium. Depending on the lawyer's competency and reputation, this in itself might be enough to tilt the balance of power in favor of the injured party. While the short-term effect is to give the claimant a boost, the lawyer and the insurance company know that the game has only just begun.

After the claimant's lawyer generates several offers and counteroffers, the insurance company makes its last and final offer. Normally, the final offer is well below the amount demanded. At this point, the enticement of the check in hand coupled with the uncertainty of forthcoming litigation will cause many clients and lawyers to accept the "purported" final offer. On the other hand, it must be pointed out that accepting an insurance company's offer at this stage might be prudent, depending on the facts surrounding a case.

In our example, if the claimant's lawyer allowed the insurance company to maintain control throughout the early stages of the negotiation, the last and final offer will be quick in coming and low in amount. Alternatively, if the claimant's counsel has maintained a balance of power, the insurance company will be much slower in issuing an ultimatum and, when it does, the amount will be greater than in situations where control has been lost. If the balance of power has been tilted in favor of one negotiator for an extended period of time, odds are that this negotiator will usually be the one making the final settlement offer—not receiving it.

§ 6.23 Balancing and Counterbalancing

It is important to recognize the role that balancing played in this personal injury scenario. At the beginning of the negotiation, the injured party's expectation level was extremely high due to emotionalism, unrealistic perceptions, and misinformation. Consequently, the insurance company enjoyed a power advantage at this stage because of its superior knowledge and experience. The company's position was reflected by its low settlement offer to the injured party. Subsequently, the injured party was able to strengthen his position by retaining a lawyer and thus acquiring additional information and knowledge about the settlement process.

In essence, the injured party was able to bring the balance of power back into a state of equilibrium or balance. The balance of power tilted in favor of the insurance company when it made its last and final offer. The injured party and his lawyer were subjected to the enticement of the alleged last chance to settle without having to engage in costly and time-consuming litigation.

Let us assume the injured party and his lawyer called the insurance company's bluff and the injured party instituted suit. Upon filing suit, the balance of power was restored and possibly tilted in favor of the plaintiff, depending on the specific law and facts involved. This balancing process continued with filing responsive pleadings and trial motions and taking depositions. Throughout the process, the parties' confidence levels were subjected to a continued ebb and flow that was ultimately reflected in the bottom line of the final settlement agreement.

§ 6.24 The Importance of Controlling Intensity

The ability to control the intensity of a negotiation is often as important as the ability to control the pace of the bargaining process. Consider the control strategy of a union labor leader seeking to negotiate a new agreement with management. At their first meeting, the labor leader announces his intention to call a strike if an agreement cannot be reached before a specified deadline. Such a ploy is a highly intensive way of attempting to gain and maintain control over the bargaining process. The union's position could be further intensified by announcing the proposed strike at a press conference held immediately before the opening meeting with management. Here, the labor leader has used intensity to dramatize his union's demands and to rally the support of the rank and file. It also has the effect of drawing the battle lines with the opposition. While such an approach can represent an intensive and provocative approach to negotiation, there are times when the circumstances require this type of aggression.

In contrast to this highly intensive approach, consider the situation of a diplomat of a strategically important, nonaligned, Third World nation attempting to gain support for a sensitive proposition advocated by his country. Here, the circumstances call for a more oblique approach to bargaining to avoid the negative fallout from an adverse reaction. Lowering the intensity level is a vital consideration that will affect how the diplomat approaches his task.

Lawyers use these two intensity extremes and everything in between on a daily basis. The typical example of a low-intensity control tactic is a letter suggesting a course of action that is not backed up with any threat of suit or deadline for action. Conversely, a demand letter incorporating a threat of suit along with a "short fuse" deadline (10 days or less) illustrates the use of a more intensive control tactic. The lawyer's ability to read a situation and respond with the appropriate intensity will go a long way in affecting the bottom-line success or failure of the negotiation.

§ 6.25 Controlling Focus to Keep the Negotiation on Track

A third target for control is the focus of the negotiation. How many times have you been engaged in a conversation with friends only to see the subject of the discussion meander repeatedly? This phenomenon illustrates a failure of the parties to control the focus of the conversation. In most casual conversations, there is little need to control focus. In a negotiation, the ability to control focus can be of paramount importance.

Focus and the Iraq War: The best example of the importance of focus relates to the Bush administration's case for waging war in Iraq after the 9-11 attacks in 2001. The first response to the attacks centered in Afghanistan in October 2001. In late 2002 and early 2003, the President and his administration began to focus solely on Saddam Hussein's regime in Iraq. Placing the emphasis on 9-11, weapons of mass destruction, and Saddam Hussein provided the justification for the March 19, 2003, attack by the United States, Britain, and other coalition partners. Although the assertions of the Bush administration turned out to be based on erroneous intelligence, the focus on Iraq was converted into a mandate for the president.

Despite the debacle that ensued, this is a perfect illustration of the power of focus to change the status quo. The disastrous results provide an equally compelling object lesson to those who would plunge headfirst into a negotiation without thinking through the repercussions. The higher the stakes in any given negotiation, the greater the level of reflection, planning, and verification of facts that is required.

§ 6.26 Two Subtle Techniques to Help You Control Focus

Two communication techniques can be used to help you control the focus of a negotiation. They are repetition and listening. These simple and subtle techniques may be used in every conceivable negotiating situation. While both may appear of minor importance, do not be fooled. They can be very important in keeping a negotiation on track.

Even though repetition and listening are both communication techniques, they employ completely opposite approaches. Repetition is a technique used to send information. Conversely, listening is a technique used to receive information. When used together, they become an extremely powerful control device. Let us examine each in more detail.

§ 6.27 Repetition, Repetition, Repetition

During a complex negotiation, it is not uncommon for the negotiators to become bogged down discussing collateral issues. As any family law practitioner will attest, parties to a domestic dispute often lose sight of their main objective—getting a divorce—and make every collateral point a deal point. Trying to reach a negotiated settlement when the parties subordinate their main objective each time a secondary issue is confronted can be a nightmare. Repetition is an effective way to control such situations.

Repetition can help the negotiator do two things: (1) Focus your opponent on your objective, and (2) Emphasize your strong points or your opponent's weak points.

Repetition reminds. Consequently, both the sender and receiver are constantly reminded of the primary issue at hand. Repetition keeps your main objective foremost in your opponent's mind, making it much more difficult for primary issues to be sidetracked.

Successful use of repetition requires subtlety. It should not be employed by repeating standard phrases in a mechanical manner. Instead, the desired point or issue should be injected throughout the negotiation by subtle as well as obvious statements. When repetition is used properly, your opponent should have no doubt as to the issues that comprise the parameters of the negotiation.

Repetition also serves to emphasize and reinforce. Both plaintiff and defense attorneys use repetition during trial to emphasize to the judge or jury the strengths of their case or the weaknesses of their opponent's case. The repeated reminders of one's strengths or an opponent's weaknesses have a persuasive effect not only on the judge or jury but also on the opponent.

Repetition can also be used as a way to exert the leverage of uncertainty over an opponent. After being told of the weaknesses of a case, everyone, including your opponent, may begin to believe it. For instance, consider settlement negotiations involving a personal injury claim. The first move any defense lawyer usually makes is to tell opposing counsel why the plaintiff does not have a strong enough case to merit the amount demanded. The defense attorney will magnify his opponent's weak points while emphasizing the client's strong points to cause doubt and uncertainty in the opponent. Repetition is useful in promoting uncertainty in the opposition's position throughout the negotiation.

§ 6.28 The Art of Listening

Listening is another helpful communication technique that can be used to control the focus of a negotiation. It takes concentrated effort to listen closely to what someone is saying. There is a tendency to interject a comment or idea without letting the person who is talking complete her statement. As a result, the would-be listener spends more time preparing a response than he does listening to what the speaker has to say. Consequently, the listener fails to hear a portion of the message. This opens the door to misunderstandings and problems rather than to solutions.

Real listening requires disciplined concentration. This can prove to be a considerable challenge. Developing good listening habits will allow you to ferret out relevant information and ask probing questions designed to cut through the verbiage and get to the problem. Sustained active listening is by no means easy, but it is essential to your success as a communicator. Failure to listen actively is the quickest way to let the negotiation's focus stray to secondary issues or, worse yet, to issues you have no interest in pursuing.

Even if the negotiation stays focused on the issues you consider important, failure to listen to and understand the other side will impede your ability to reach workable solutions acceptable to all concerned.

7

Tactical Negotiating Ploys That Can Improve Your Bargaining Position

Every negotiation is characterized by moves and countermoves designed to advance the process to a successful conclusion. We refer to these tactical moves and countermoves as "ploys." Some prove to be highly effective; others do not. A major reason for success or lack thereof is the presence or absence of a strategic plan employed by the negotiator.

Consistently successful negotiators are adept at using ploys designed to achieve specific, predetermined objectives that were conceived in the prenegotiation preparation phase. This chapter is devoted to discussing those specific measures or "ploys" that will breathe life into your strategic negotiation plan, starting today.

§ 7.01 Deadlines: The Basis for Many Effective Tactical Ploys

Deadlines are the basis for a number of effective tactical ploys. Deadlines motivate people to take action. As deadlines near, pressure mounts and decisions become mandatory. Action is required. Due to the nature of the legal system, lawyers are constantly working under the pressure of deadlines. Whether a deadline is imposed by a court or an opponent, it effectively pushes cases and transactions toward conclusion.

As lawyers quickly learn, some deadlines are extremely flexible, while others are rigid and uncompromising. For example, an appeal deadline imposed by a state statute is certainly a deadline that must be taken seriously. This kind of deadline will keep a lawyer in the office late at night and over the weekend. On the other hand, an informal deadline imposed in a demand letter from an opponent that threatens suit unless some action is taken by a certain date is a flexible time demand that would not normally cause as great a degree of concern.

§ 7.02 Deadlines in Action

Deadlines are useful in promoting action because they exert pressure on the negotiating process. For instance, assume you want to apply maximum pressure on an opponent. This can be accomplished by setting deadlines that are regulated by the court or some other independent authority that will have ultimate control over determination of the case. Once a deadline is set in accordance with the rules of the court or other authority, you can level maximum pressure at your opponent by simply refusing to consent to her request to alter the timetable. In most instances, lawyers are liberal in granting voluntary extensions of time and other procedural modifications to opponents when such action is permissible. But in those situations where the objective is to apply maximum pressure on your opponent, remain steadfast and refuse to modify the official rules. While such action will undoubtedly eliminate the possibility of reciprocal favors from your opponent, it will subject her to a pressurized situation, causing her to act. Such action is likely to be to your advantage.

PRACTICE TIP: For maximum effect, couple your deadline demand with sanctions imposed by some higher authority. If the deadline is not adhered to, remain firm in your stand and allow the sanction to be imposed.

§ 7.03 Informal Deadlines

Lawyers use informal deadlines regularly in their dealings with opposing counsel and clients. An informal deadline is a pronouncement by one party that some specified action be taken within a stated time period. Informal deadlines are imposed or dictated by the opposition in an effort to advance the case toward resolution. If these demands are not satisfied, the party making the demand promises to respond with some type of sanction. Basically, there are two forms of informal deadlines—the short-fuse and the flexible deadline.

§ 7.04 Short-Fuse Deadlines

If your objective is to spark immediate action, attach a short fuse to your deadline. For example, instead of giving the opposing party 30 days to respond to your demand letter, shorten the fuse to 10 days or less. To enhance the credibility of your deadline, be prepared at the time the deadline is announced to take the threatened action immediately if response is not made within the given time. For instance, when writing a demand letter in connection with a contract breach, advise the defaulting party he has "10 days to remedy the default or the attached lawsuit will be filed." The party realizes that the threat of suit is real. Why? Because your opponent can see the complaint that will include a demand for attorney fees, pre-and post-judgment interest and court costs, in addition to the principal amount due your client. The attached complaint legitimizes the deadline threat. The work has already been done. Pressure mounts. The opponent realizes that inaction will result in suit being filed. To avoid suit, the opponent will have to act.

Using short-fuse deadlines brings a sense of immediacy to the imposed deadline. Whenever possible, support your threat with some documentation indicating that you will take action if the deadline is not met. The short fuse should never exceed 10 days; otherwise, it will lose its effectiveness. Allowing the opponent too much time defuses the power of the deadline. Time releases pressure; thus, the sense of urgency will be sacrificed. This is why the fuse must remain short.

PRACTICE TIP: To enhance short-fuse deadlines, keep the response time to 10 days or less and always be prepared to follow through with your threat immediately if the deadline is not met.

---

§ 7.05 Flexible Deadlines

The flexible deadline is well suited for situations in which you want to press your opponent but are not yet prepared to take drastic action. The flexible deadline is imposed by extending the opponent's response time beyond 10 days (e.g., 14 days, 30 days, 90 days) or by using language in the demand designed to promote flexibility. Phrases such as "in the near future," "it is necessary to resolve this problem shortly," and "let me hear from you regarding this matter" do not box in an opponent. Instead, flexibility is promoted and exchange is solicited. The flexible deadline serves to put the recipient on notice of the existence of the problem and establishes the need for a response without setting a rigid time limit.

The flexible deadline is especially useful in situations that require diplomacy or in those instances where you are not sure you have all the facts and want to engage in a dialogue with your opponent.

It is important to discriminate between those situations truly requiring an uncompromising approach and those in which flexibility should be exhibited. Be cautious not to take inflexible deadline positions continually without documenting your threat and following through if the deadline is not met. Otherwise, you stand to lose all credibility. Flexible deadlines are useful ploys to help you position your case without drawing a hard line. They are a moderate alternative to short-fuse deadline demands.

You Have Until Sundown: The power of a deadline to provoke action depends on its credibility. An excellent example of a highly credible deadline is April 15. Every year, last-minute taxpayers furiously fill out forms and scribble out checks to the Treasury Department in an effort to beat the midnight filing deadline. But why? The reason has to do with credibility.

The Internal Revenue Service spends a great deal of time and money to promote the image that it will relentlessly pursue people who fail to send in their returns on time. The IRS's arsenal of weapons includes expensive and time-consuming audits as well as assessment of penalties, interest and, in extreme situations, criminal prosecutions and seizure of assets. The fear the IRS has implanted in the American psyche with its April 15 deadline ensures compliance by the overwhelming number of law-abiding taxpayers who quake at the thought of an April 16 postmark on their return.

Three Ways to Insulate Yourself from Deadline Pressure: Deadlines are a fact of life. Everyone is subject to them, but that doesn't mean you are helpless against them The best way to offset the power of a deadline is to take steps to insulate yourself from it.

The first step to shielding yourself from pressure is to discover your opponent's deadline for action and then take steps to ensure it is not yours. Second, armed with the knowledge that everything takes longer than you think it will, cushion your actual deadline with as much extra time as you can. Third, never announce your real deadline. Of course, it is not always feasible to escape being victimized by a deadline. However, these are measures that can minimize the downside of a disadvantageous deadline.

§ 7.06 Demanding a Premium for Immediate Satisfaction

Many cases are settled because of an absence of supporting facts or documentation, lack of provable damages, unfavorable case law, or poor jury verdict expectancy. Another factor to consider in settlement negotiations is the acuteness of the client's immediate needs. How soon must your client close the deal? Is the opposing party under serious time or financial pressures to settle? Can your client afford to outwait the opposition?

In many situations involving corporations, financial institutions, and insurance companies, the time value of money becomes an overriding factor that will induce the client to pay a premium for immediate satisfaction. Settlements often revolve around the reality that a dollar paid or received today will not carry the same value next month or next year. Consequently, settlement decisions are often tied to sheer dollars-and-cents pragmatics with legal considerations playing a secondary role.

§ 7.07 Impatience

Litigating a lawsuit from beginning to end is a long, arduous task for both lawyer and client. The legal system offers defendants numerous places to hide within its complex machinery. Even if the plaintiff is fortunate enough to overcome the many hurdles raised by the defense, the prospect of an appeal still looms. Protracted litigation is expensive and time consuming. The potential rewards for the plaintiff must outweigh these downside considerations. Even if the client is willing to assume the risk of a court fight, he must also be capable of going the distance. Most are not. This is why demanding a premium for immediate satisfaction is a frequently used and often successful settlement ploy.

The success of this tactic rests on the fact that most clients are impatient. They do not understand the legal system and are astounded by how long it takes for a case to be adjudicated fully. Clients usually want their lawyers to wave a magic wand and extract immediate satisfaction measured in dollars. In reality, this seldom happens. Exploiting this common phenomenon is the essence of demanding a premium for immediate satisfaction. This ploy applies to business transactions as well as lawsuit negotiations.

§ 7.08 Taking the Easy Way Out

By recognizing the needs of the opposition, you can structure settlement offers to give immediate satisfaction in return for a premium concession. Consider the following example:

Lawyer Right represents a client who has a case that is potentially worth $100,000. The defense lawyer does not share the plaintiff's assessment as to the value of the case. The only way Lawyer Right and his client will find out if their case is truly worth $100,000 is to litigate.

Lawyer Right is confident and excited about moving the case forward. He is motivated by the professional challenge of litigation and the prospect of a substantial recovery even though it will probably be several years in materializing. Lawyer Right's client is in a different situation. The uncertainty of the legal process causes him great concern. The truth is, Lawyer Right's client is scared to death that years of litigation may result in no recovery. To make matters worse, the client needs money now. He wants and needs tangible results as soon as possible.

Lawyer Right's opponent is Lawyer Slow, a cagey old defense lawyer who is wise in the ways of human nature and the litigation process. Lawyer Slow assures Lawyer Right that there will be a long, drawn-out fight with appeals at every level if necessary. But, if Lawyer Right's client would be willing to accept a much lower settlement amount to avoid the hazards of litigation, then maybe "something could be worked out."

Lawyer Right and his client now confront a question frequently raised in negotiations between lawyers and their clients: whether to accept a fixed sum certain today even though it will be substantially lower than what might be recovered sometime in the future. In short, whether to pay a premium for immediate satisfaction of present needs.

In the overwhelming majority of cases, clients prefer to control their destiny and opt for certainty over uncertainty. Premiums are thus paid to satisfy the client's immediate financial needs. The lower settlement amount eliminates the client's psychological concerns, and the client trades the certainty of a reduced settlement for the uncertainty of litigation.

A client's or opponent's demand for immediate satisfaction is analogous to a discount factor. If the potential value of a case is $100,000, the only way the plaintiff will possibly recover that amount is to jump through the seemingly endless hoops of the legal system. To avoid this unpleasant and time-consuming experience, the potential value of the case is discounted.

This scenario is played out daily. It is based on an exploitation of the plaintiff's lack of willingness and capability to persevere and press on into the perilous and uncertain future.

§ 7.09 Applying the Same Ploy to Business Negotiations

Immediate satisfaction is often used in business negotiations. Transactions involving cash down payments and long-term financing are prime examples. The purchase price is often discounted in return for a larger cash down payment. Regardless of the strength of the collateral securing a long-term purchase agreement, there is always a chance of problems arising. In other words, there is always uncertainty. Cash paid today is certain. It satisfies immediate needs and alleviates uncertainty. This is simply another application of paying a premium for immediate satisfaction.

PRACTICE TIP: When you are in a position to give the other party immediate satisfaction, be sure to extract a premium in return.

---

§ 7.10 Using Surprise as an Effective Negotiating Tactic

Generally, lawyers guard against surprises. Very rarely is a surprise viewed as something positive.

Accordingly, lawyers invest hours of preparation time prior to a negotiation or trial. Unfortunately, no matter how thoroughly a lawyer prepares, surprises will still surface from time to time. When surprises do occur and you are fortunate enough to be in a position to take advantage of an unexpected turn of events, do not hesitate to do so.

§ 7.11 Surprise: The Offensive Perspective

When a startling bit of information presents itself, the natural urge is to use it immediately in hope of securing a quick knockout punch.

In actuality, this is rarely the result. It is more likely that the announcement of some surprising news will be brushed aside by the opposition as inconsequential, equalized in short order, or simply ignored. Instead of squandering surprise information on unproductive dramatics, it should be used as a catalyst or tool to advance and develop an existing strategy or tactic. When used in a deliberate fashion, surprise information serves to accelerate you toward your objective.

For example, assume you are engaged in a negotiation with another lawyer over the question of whether a contract between your respective clients is enforceable. Your opponent confidently recites all the reasons why your client will be held responsible if the case proceeds to trial. His objective, of course, is to increase your uncertainty and thus increase the settlement value of his case. Your adversary's approach is correct in all respects, except for his failure to uncover vital information in the form of a recently decided state Supreme Court case that substantially weakens his legal position. The natural temptation is to interrupt him and say, "I suggest you review the recently decided XYZ case. After you read it, you'll see that your position has no merit." However, there is a better approach.

Let your opponent tell you all the reasons why his client should recover. Hear him out. After he has revealed his entire case, attempt to subordinate all other arguments to case law. Force the opposing lawyer to adopt case law as the primary basis for his demands. After he has concluded current case law that supports his position, inject some uncertainty. "Well, I think what you're saying would probably be right under the old line of cases, but didn't the Supreme Court change all that in a recent decision? Let me check on it and I'll be back in touch."

You can be sure your opponent will read the case within the hour and learn the unfortunate news for himself. After a few days, you can follow with a letter stating that "in view of the recent Supreme Court ruling in the XYZ case, we feel your previous position will, by necessity, be subject to reappraisal. Nonetheless, we will be glad to work with you to resolve this matter in short order. To do so, we propose the following action...."

Caution: Surprises can backfire. Never lose sight of your objective—the permanent resolution of your client's problem. The key word is *permanent*. Surprises hurled at an opponent may give you a short-term advantage. However, in the long run, using surprise against an opponent will create distrust, impair communication, and motivate your opponent to prolong the dispute to save face even if there is little chance of ultimate success. Nobody likes to have a smug opponent point out shortcomings, errors, and weaknesses. It is not smart negotiation.

To avoid these problems and still derive permanent maximum benefits, help your opponent arrive at the inescapable conclusion initiated by your surprise information. The effect will be less dramatic but much more profitable for your client.

§ 7.12 Surprise: The Defensive Perspective

Unwanted surprises can manifest themselves in a number of ways. New demands, presentation of new issues, shortened deadlines, irrational arguments, or the discovery of shocking information damaging to your client's position are the most common examples. Even though a negotiator prepares thoroughly, she is still subject to the unexpected. Delay is the key to fending off an opponent's use of surprise. Any maneuver designed to buy time will help soften the impact of surprise. In most cases, once you have gained enough time to analyze and adjust to the new information, you can cope with most surprises by taking steps to neutralize the short-term advantage gained by the opposition.

§ 7.13 Patience: One of the Most Powerful Weapons in the Negotiator's Arsenal

Americans by their nature are impatient. This national character trait has a direct bearing on the way American lawyers negotiate with one another and with lawyers from other countries. Typically, American lawyers are viewed by their counterparts in other countries as always being impatient. Conversely, Americans tend to view most foreign lawyers as being lackadaisical, with little concern for getting immediate results. As a general rule, it is difficult for American negotiators to demonstrate patience unless they have been through many bargaining sessions. Patience is a learned virtue. It develops with maturity and experience.

Patience is one of the most powerful ploys in the negotiator's arsenal. Potentially, it is the ultimate ploy. The negotiator who develops the ability to absorb tension without submitting to the pressures of premature settlement is an adversary to be respected. The exercise of patience can rob the opposition of his superiority in facts, law, and leverage.

The advantages that flow from using patience as a ploy are grounded in the leverage of timing. The patient negotiator is always in a position to maximize timing opportunities throughout a negotiation. Patience leads to:

- Concessions;
- Reduction of an opponent's expectation level;
- Discovery of new alternatives; and
- Desirable settlements.

When two, equally matched negotiators enter into bargaining, the one exhibiting the most patience will usually prevail.

> ***Practice Tip:*** Quick settlements that prove unsatisfactory are usually the result of poor judgment and lack of patience on the part of one of the negotiators.

§ 7.14 Affirmative Inaction: When the Best Move is No Move

Periodically, you will find yourself in situations where the best move is no move. That is, simply do nothing. We refer to the ploys used in these situations as "affirmative inaction." There are four basic types of affirmative inaction:

1. Going silent.
2. Ground zero—your move.
3. Let the situation deteriorate.
4. Collapse.

§ 7.15 Going Silent

Lawyers love to talk. As a group, they find it difficult to control their urge to speak up, even in situations where communication is damaging. The skilled negotiator, however, is the exception to the rule. Skilled negotiators know when and why to go silent.

There are numerous instances when silence may be used as an active negotiating ploy.

Expand your knowledge base: Consider the situation where you do not have all the facts. You know that, due to missing information, your grasp of the case is fuzzy and uncertain. Silence can be used as an affirmative inaction ploy to increase your knowledge base. By soliciting information from your opponent and encouraging her to talk, you will permit the opposition to disclose vital aspects about the negotiation. Chances are your opponent will reveal more information than necessary. When this happens, so much the better for you.

Silence and depositions: Silence is used as a ploy to gain information from opposing parties and witnesses at depositions. The trick is to construct short, direct questions and then back off, letting the witness ramble. The less you interrupt, the better. The witness feels he is carrying the conversation and, therefore, must say something to keep the discussion alive. The result is a successful deposition; a transcript filled with pages of testimony from the witness—not questions from the lawyer. To achieve this result, you must consciously suppress your desire to engage in argument or dialogue. Go silent and let the witness do the talking.

Silence as a shield: In situations where the opposition is engaged in a verbal battle with you, simply go silent. Silence neutralizes this type of opponent quickly. Your opponent will soon run out of steam, especially if he is failing to get a reaction from you. The opponent's staccato pace cannot be maintained without resting points that are supplied when you intervene with a response. Remain silent and let your opponent wear down and out.

Silence helps you play it close: Silence is an excellent ploy for restricting the amount of information you want passed to the other side. This is especially true in situations in which you are attempting to camouflage a weak position. Silence helps you disguise the soft spots. By limiting the amount of information you broadcast to the other side, you decrease the chance of the opponent's discovering and exploiting your weaknesses.

Silence is not avoidance: Do not confuse silence with avoidance. Silence is affirmative inaction. There should always be a reason for your failure to speak or act. An experienced negotiator using silence as a ploy will outwardly appear to be open and will likely be very accommodating when a request is made to hold a meeting or to engage in a telephone conversation. The reason will most likely be that your opponent wants information from you. To achieve this result, your opponent will put the burden of carrying the discussion squarely on you while he simply sits back and listens. If you are on the wrong side of a one-way conversation, beware.

PRACTICE TIP: Silence is like a magnet. It attracts information without divulging any in return. When you go silent, know why and make a point to listen.

---

§ 7.16 Ground Zero—Your Move

This ploy rests on the basic fact that all cases start at ground zero. To move past this point, the plaintiff's lawyer must take action. The first step may be a phone call, demand letter, a lawsuit, or some other initiative. In most situations, the defense lawyer is in an excellent position to use this ploy. Unless the opposition makes a move, the case stays at ground zero. Your ploy is simply to do nothing until the other side moves from ground zero. By the time the opposition moves the case (e.g., by filing a lawsuit), you can return it to ground zero with a balancing move (e.g., by filing an answer). The next move is your opponent's.

For example, consider the insurance defense lawyer who is threatened with a lawsuit. The parties start at ground zero. The initial and most cost-effective ploy by the defense lawyer is simply to do nothing. Unless suit is actually filed, nothing more will be required. Often, the lawsuit never comes. Money never changes hands on the strength of empty threats. It was up to the plaintiff's lawyer to press the claim and move the case off ground zero. He never did. The defendant wins.

§ 7.17 Let the Situation Deteriorate

Sometimes your position is improved when the situation gets worse. For instance, consider the plight of a minority stockholder who has attempted to get corporate management to hold annual stockholder meetings, to no avail. Notice of demand to hold annual meetings is sent to corporate management, but still no action is taken. In addition, corporate management also ignores the notice of demand to furnish the minority stockholder financial statements. With each refusal, the minority shareholder believes that his situation looks bleaker—or does it? To the contrary, as the situation gets worse, the minority stockholder's case gets stronger. Corporate management's consistent and obstinate refusal to afford the minority shareholder his basic rights under the corporate bylaws will ultimately cement the stockholder's legal position and be the undoing of management. The case against corporate management was good after the first refusal, better after the second, and even better after the third.

§ 7.18 Collapse

The collapse ploy, sometimes called the Cleopatra defense, may be used in situations when you want to avoid battle or confrontation at all costs. Consider the following example.

A small family-owned business finds itself in an unmanageable financial bind. It becomes apparent that the business cannot survive. The only way to avoid continuing losses, which will ultimately lead to bankruptcy, is to liquidate the business, pay off creditors, and close down. All factors indicate that liquidation is the most desirable alternative under the circumstances, except for one.

Unfortunately, the business has just renewed its lease agreement for another six-year term. To make matters worse, the lease has been guaranteed by personal endorsements of the owners. As the lawyer for this small business, you are faced with the following points to consider:

- The client has ruled out bankruptcy as an alternative.
- The new lease agreement is valid and enforceable in all respects.
- The landlord is financially strong and respected in the community.
- The tenant is extremely weak financially.
- Liquidation will barely pay all outstanding debts and other expenses.
- The individual owners have no assets from which to draw funds to make a settlement proposal to the landlord or to engage in litigation.

Your primary objective is to convince the landlord to voluntarily rescind the lease agreement. Keeping in mind that your client has no money to fund a settlement proposal or to spend on litigation that he would most likely lose, the consequences are obvious. You are at the landlord's mercy. How do you go about convincing the landlord to voluntarily cancel the lease? The answer: Collapse.

The value of collapse stems from neutralizing the hostility present in most lawsuits. Lawsuits are spawned by parties who have antagonized one another. If hostility between the parties is high, lawsuits normally emerge as a natural consequence. Collapse is designed to remove or reduce hostility so that litigation can be avoided and settlement reached.

The conversation with the landlord would go something like this:

My clients are extremely upset about having to close down their business. As you know, they have been in business for over nine years. But during the last 18 months, they have been forced to realize that the business cannot continue. They simply must liquidate now before the situation gets completely out of hand. At present, bankruptcy is not an alternative. My clients are fully aware that you have the capability and right to drag them through court over this lease agreement. They certainly have no desire to fight with someone with whom they have had such a good relationship for so long. As embarrassing as it is for my clients, they are asking for your help.

This approach eliminates all hostility, even though the tenant is going to have to default on the lease agreement. The lawyer fully admits that the landlord has the ability and right to sue his clients. But, while admitting these points, he asks for help. It is very difficult for hostility to emerge between two parties when one party is sincerely asking for help. Collapse is a request to the opposition to show mercy. It is much easier for a strong opponent to rationalize leniency if the opponent generally likes the person requesting help.

Practice Tip: Lawsuits are normally spawned by parties who have antagonized one another to the point of open hostility. Collapse attempts to eliminate the hostility factor and avoid litigation.

§ 7.19 Demands: A Key to Understanding the Negotiating Process

Everyone is subject to demands, especially lawyers. Letters, phone calls, and lawsuits are all vehicles for the countless demands and counterdemands that are a natural part of any lawyer's practice. Demands can range from outrageous ultimatums to fair requests to empty bluffs. Formulating and reacting to demands comprises much of a lawyer's practice. Because the substance and manner in which a demand is made can have a pronounced effect on a negotiation, it is important that you develop an appreciation and understanding of demands.

§ 7.20 The Demand Pattern Formula: No. Why? Too High

The initial reaction to most demands in legal negotiation is "No." As time passes and the negotiators exchange information and develop a working relationship, the "no" response usually mellows to a

"Why?"—"Why do you think that your demand is fair?" "Why do you need that particular point?" Eventually, "Why?" turns to "Too high"—"You are asking for too much." So, the typical response pattern to demands is "No. Why? Too high." If you are the negotiator issuing the demand, your response to counterproposals generally will follow the same pattern: "No. Why? Too low."

As negotiations proceed, this pattern is repeated until the gap separating the negotiators is finally bridged. If the gap is not closed by negotiation, a business deal never materializes or, in the case of a legal claim, litigation ensues.

§ 7.21 Using Credible Uncertainty to Bridge the Gap

When it comes time to make a demand, most lawyers fall into a common trap. They either structure their demands unrealistically high, making substantive negotiation impossible or unfeasible. Or they make the demand too low, thereby seriously devaluing their case. In both instances, the demands lose impact. Neither excess creates credible uncertainty in the mind of the opposition. Before we look at how to use credible uncertainty in structuring demands, let us first examine these two traps in more detail.

§ 7.22 Shoot for the Moon

This trap occurs when one side makes a ridiculous demand that will almost always be viewed by the opposition as absurd. Even though chances are slim that such a demand will ever be effective, many negotiators try it on the off chance that it might work. Their reasoning is simple: You never know until you ask. The worst the other side can do is say no. We can always lower our sights later. As a result, shooting for the moon is a frequently used tactic.

§ 7.23 Leaving Money on the Table

Conversely, when your demand is too low, you run the risk of having the offer snapped up, leaving money on the table. Alternatively, if the offer is not taken seriously, you jeopardize the final settlement amount. When this happens, the opposition will perceive your position as one of weakness. A low initial demand will quickly devalue your case in the eyes of your opponent. As happens in the shoot-for-the-moon trap, the low demand fails to create any uncertainty. As a result, it does not receive serious consideration.

§ 7.24 Credible Uncertainty: The Key to Making Effective Demands

The key to making good demands is to maintain a balance between shooting for the moon and leaving money on the table. You want to make a demand that will invoke maximum credible uncertainty. For example, assume you have been retained to represent a client who has been injured in a minor automobile accident. Assume you have concluded that a fair settlement range is $5,000 to $7,000. However, if the case goes to trial, you have determined that potential jury verdict expectancy would be in the $10,000 to $12,000 range. What should your opening demand be?

If you demand $100,000, would this invoke uncertainty in the mind of the opposition? No. The defense lawyer has access to the same jury verdict expectancy charts. He knows that his maximum exposure is only $12,000 if, in fact, you push the case to trial. Your demand for $100,000 would be ignored.

On the other hand, assume you offer to settle the case for $1,000. Such a demand would indicate to your opponent that you do not know the value of your case and probably do not know what you are doing. Your opponent will either accept your offer or ignore it. In either event, you lose.

§ 7.25 How to Create Credible Uncertainty

Consider making a demand of $9,750. This amount invokes credible uncertainty in the opposition. They are compelled to consider your demand. Because the demand is lower than the probable jury verdict, the defense must determine whether its case is strong enough to avoid a jury verdict higher than the settlement offer. The defense has a decision to make. Though they will likely make a counteroffer, the negotiation process has begun. The parties' respective positions begin to narrow as a result of the credible certainty of the plaintiff's demand.

§ 7.26 Boost Your Offer for Later Concessions

Once you determine the optimum range for invoking credible uncertainty in the opposition, add an additional amount to be used as trade points. You know from the demand pattern that regardless of the amount of your first demand, the response from the opposition will almost always be negative. When you reach stage two and your opponent is asking why you think the amount demanded is fair, you will be in a credible position to tell your opponent.

To calculate a demand that will create credible uncertainty, you must first consider proof problems, applicable law, and jury verdict expectancy. All of these elements help you substantiate why your demand is fair. When you reach stage three of the demand pattern—too high—the extra amount you added at the outset will provide you with trade points you can concede to the opposition without discounting the true value of your claim.

The demand-counterdemand pattern will continue back and forth with each side adjusting its demand up or down depending on the circumstances affecting the case. By carefully considering the amount of your initial demand and basing it on fact rather than wishful thinking, you will put yourself in a much better position to play this game successfully.

PRACTICE TIP: Structure your demands to expose your opponents to maximum credible uncertainty.

§ 7.27 Beware of Bracketing

You should always be aware that each demand or counterdemand acts to constrain the negotiators. We refer to this as "bracketing." This is the principle behind the floor/ceiling trap previously discussed. To illustrate, assume you originally offer to settle a case for $25,000. The opposition counters with $2,000; you counteroffer $15,000. The negotiation is now confined to the $15,000 to $2,000 range. In this instance, the brackets have worked in favor of the negotiator making the $2,000 offer of settlement. Why? This negotiator's exposure has been reduced from $25,000 to $15,000 for a mere $2,000 in return. The defense lawyer has reduced his uncertainty level at the equivalent rate of 20 cents on the dollar. Not bad.

§ 7.28 Avoid Getting Trapped

Bracketing can work to the benefit of both sides in that it helps narrow the issues and amount in controversy. But beware that you do not become trapped within too small an area. This situation frequently occurs in negotiations between insurance adjusters and lawyers, where the primary issue generally comes down to money.

Normally in this type of settlement negotiation, plaintiff's counsel will submit an itemization of all medical expenses and other damages in support of the total demand. The initial reaction from the adjuster is one of shock (the "no" phase of the demand pattern). After the typical exchange of information and explanation of certain facts, the "why?" phase of the demand pattern is completed.

Next comes the attempt to bracket-in plaintiff's counsel. The adjuster may say, "Let's see if we can settle this case. How much do you really think it's worth? Give me a fair demand and I'll see what I can do to dispose of this file." Beware, the tendency is to be fair, just, and reasonable and say, "Well, we would be willing to take X amount." At this point, you have been bracketed between the amount the insurance company previously offered and your quotation. The case will probably not settle at your fair and reasonable amount. Instead, negotiations will continue in an attempt to reduce the actual amount even further below your settlement target.

To fully understand the implications of the adjuster's knowing your actual assessment of the claim's value, consider the reverse. What if you as plaintiff's lawyer could ask the same question of the insurance adjuster and get an answer. "Well, after much thought, the company thinks the claim is really worth $20,000." How helpful would this information be from your standpoint as the plaintiff's negotiator?

§ 7.29 Keep Your Demands Flexible

To avoid the pitfall of bracketing, try to keep your demands flexible. For instance, you could respond to an adjuster seeking to bracket you with, "Well, I truly believe our case is worth exactly what I asked for in our initial demand because of the reasons I've already stated. Nonetheless, I would be willing to recommend to my client that we discount this amount in return for an expedited settlement. It's really up to you as to how much we might be willing to discount depending on how long you want to delay settlement of the case."

Even though a settlement range will emerge, the brackets are flexible. The negotiator is still in a good position to seek a settlement without being confined to a limited settlement area in the event discussions break down.

§ 7.30 The Advantages of Limited Authority

The last thing a negotiator wants to do is announce to an opponent that she has full authority to settle a case. A negotiator's best ally is the cloak of limited authority. The negotiator vested with limited authority has three distinct advantages over the negotiator empowered with full authority.

§ 7.31 Limited Authority: The Negotiator's Back Door

First, limited authority gives you the option to avoid making decisions whenever it suits you. It becomes the negotiator's back door. No matter what kind of predicament you face, you can always defer making a decision until you have had the opportunity to confer with your principal, client, boss, or whomever. How many times have you heard another lawyer say, "Let me check with my client and I'll get back to you about your settlement offer"?

The ploy of limited authority is used throughout the business world to insulate against spontaneous or reactionary decisions. Insurance adjusters always seem to have to check with their regional supervisors before concluding a settlement; bank loan officers always have to refer a request to the loan committee; corporate officers consult their boards of directors; government officials must seek the approval of their department heads.

Limited authority insulates the negotiator. It is a legitimate means around an aggressive opponent who is pressing for an on-the-spot decision. This can provide a definite advantage when faced with a pressurized situation requiring an immediate decision.

§ 7.32 Limited Authority Justifies a Higher Authority

Limited authority also provides you with the excuse to bring in another negotiator, or a higher authority. For instance, assume you announced at the beginning of a negotiation that you have limited authority. Further assume that talks reach a standstill several weeks later. In order to move the talks forward, you can inform your opponent that the client, senior partner, or some other higher authority will attend the next session in an effort to resolve the problem. This maneuver would not be possible had you stated at the outset that the decision to settle was solely up to you.

§ 7.33 Limited Authority Insulates the Real Decision Maker

Additionally, in cases involving limited authority, the real decision maker is insulated from the heat of the battle. It affords the person making the final decision, usually the client, to do so purely on fact, without becoming swayed by personality or emotional considerations.

While a negotiator never wants to reveal that he has full authority, the opposite is true for the opponent. You always want to deal with someone who has full authority. There are two reasons. First, unless you are negotiating with the real decision maker, everything you say in support of your position will be filtered before it reaches the person making the final decision. In essence, you must rely on your opponent to restate your position to his superior. You become dependent on your opponent to sell your case. Rest assured, something will get lost in the translation.

Second, by dealing with someone who has limited authority, you are allowing your opponent the same "back door" to evade you when it comes time to make important decisions. Consequently, you never really know where you stand on questions requiring immediate answers. Your opponent is in a position to let the answers linger until it suits him. This is why it is essential to determine who among the opposition has decision-making authority.

PRACTICE TIP: Always have a back door to facilitate a quick getaway if needed. Limited authority will provide this back door. Use it.

---

§ 7.34 Concessions: Making a Designed Retreat

When you engage in a negotiation, you must be prepared to make concessions. Demands made during negotiations are the "take" side of bargaining; concessions are the "give" side. A timely concession made can be just as important as a concession received in concluding a negotiation. Making concessions should not be viewed negatively. Concessions are absolutely essential to making the negotiation process work. Some negotiators refer to concession-making as a "designed retreat."

§ 7.35 The Role of Trade Points

In order to know what you can concede, you must have a plan that breaks your objectives and leverage into deal points, secondary points, and trade points. This last category is where you should look first for your concessions or throwaways. These are points that you intend to give up during the negotiation. They are sometimes referred to as "straw men." The key to using trade points depends on your success in inflating their value before offering them as concessions. The more your opponent believes they are worth, the more your opponent will, in turn, concede to you.

§ 7.36 The Cardinal Rule of Making Concessions

Never make a concession unless you get something in return. Trading concessions is the classic example of the quid pro quo or something for something. We repeat, always get something in return for anything you might have given up. This rule applies equally to insignificant trade points or substantive concessions.

§ 7.37 Points to Follow When Making Concessions

Follow these guidelines when making concessions:

- Always build trade points into your negotiating plan.
- Inflate the value of your trade points.
- Confine your concessions to trade points; avoid concessions on secondary points until late in a negotiation.
- Conserve concessions. One way to increase the value of trade points is to delay conceding them until the eleventh hour.
- Pace your concession rate. Never give up too much, too fast. Make your opponent work for each concession. This will help increase the value of your trade points.
- Be aware of what you are conceding versus what you are receiving.
- Avoid giving too much away at once. Dole out concessions in little pieces. Again, this increases the value of your giveaways.
- Do not hesitate to take back a concession. Threatened concession redemption often leads to reciprocal concessions from an opponent.
- Avoid making the first concession.

Practice Tip: Never make a concession unless you get something in return.

---

§ 7.38 Persuasive Ploys: Two Techniques for Closing the Gap Between You and Your Opponent

The negotiating process is an attempt to persuade the opposition to adopt a new position closer to your own. The various moves you make throughout the bargaining process are designed to entice the opposition to close the gap toward your objective. Consequently, all moves or ploys are by their nature meant to persuade. There are two primary techniques you can use to strengthen the persuasiveness of your ploys, both of which are tied to the leverage of uncertainty.

§ 7.39 Strengthening Your Persuasive Ploys

Persuasive ploys fall into two categories: (1) those that project certainty of your position, and (2) those that create uncertainty in your opponent's position.

§ 7.40 Projecting the Certainty of Your Position

A technique for promoting certainty is the fair and reasonable man approach. It is based on the premise that you are more likely to persuade an opponent if he views you as being fair and reasonable.

One way to project this image is to substantiate your position at every possible juncture of the negotiation. Provide supporting facts, favorable case law, statutory authority, policy considerations, and positive public sentiment to substantiate your position. Substantiation leads to believability. If your opponent believes what you say, your image as being fair and reasonable is enhanced.

When a fair and reasonable person is certain of his position, uncertainty starts eroding the confidence of that person's bargaining counterpart. Your opponent is placed in the position of being viewed as unreasonable if she does not agree with you. No one wants to think of themselves as unfair or unreasonable.

The key to projecting certainty is to make the circumstances surrounding your case appear favorable to your position by substantiating and supporting your stand with objectively verifiable facts.

§ 7.41 Creating Uncertainty in Your Opponent's Position

Another approach to strengthening your persuasiveness is to design your moves in such a way as to create uncertainty in the opposition's position. A favorite ploy of skilled negotiators is to attack an opponent at the weakest point. Whether it is unfavorable case law, lack of statutory authority, or the absence of documentation or witnesses, select the weakest link and press on.

Persistently highlighting an opponent's weakness will create uncertainty in his position. By coupling this uncertainty with a confident posture, you will have exerted the maximum forward movement toward your ultimate negotiating objective.

8
The Role of Correspondence

Correspondence, if used properly, can be a key factor in getting what you want in a negotiation. We have touched briefly on other communication skills in terms of preparation and the opening move. These principles generally apply to all other phases of bargaining. This chapter focuses on a specific aspect of communication—correspondence. It discusses principles and ploys that recur frequently in the field of law-related negotiation.

§ 8.01 Correspondence Is a Key to Success

Negotiation is by no means limited to oral communication. Correspondence and other types of written communication play a vital role in most if not all negotiations in which lawyers are involved. Letters, memoranda, contract drafts, facsimiles, and e-mails are all examples of correspondence that may be used in every phase of the negotiation process, from beginning to end.

§ 8.02 The Disadvantages of Correspondence

As with the other modes of communication, certain advantages and disadvantages are associated with the use of correspondence. From a negative standpoint, correspondence is impersonal and does not lend itself to using emotional appeal. Well-thought-out correspondence takes time and effort to prepare. It tends to slow the pace of a negotiation. For most negotiators, it is simply easier to say what is on your mind than to formulate your thoughts in writing.

§ 8.03 The Advantages of Correspondence

The advantages of correspondence are numerous. Correspondence serves to put the opposing party on formal notice. It creates a permanent record of the communication. It is a powerful device for emphasizing or downplaying certain facts and positions. Correspondence is aptly designed for establishing time frames and imposing deadlines. Often, you can exert tremendous pressure on your opponent through correspondence copy power. Correspondence is a very succinct and efficient way to deliver instructions, advise of forthcoming sanctions, and focus the attention of the opposing negotiator on a desired agenda. Well-prepared correspondence is a vital aspect of the bargaining process that can be used to sway the flow of a negotiation without emotionally upsetting your opponent.

§ 8.04 A Nine-Point Plan for Writing More Powerful Demand Letters

The demand letter can serve to illustrate the skillful use of correspondence in a negotiation. All lawyers write demand letters. Frequently, the preparation of a demand letter is viewed as a perfunctory task. However, when the drafter gives demand correspondence attention, it can indeed become a powerful negotiating weapon.

The negotiator preparing a demand letter should consider the following nine points in his drafting:

1. Give proof-positive notice.
2. Educate the recipient as to the facts.

3. Highlight favorable facts.
4. Minimize damaging facts.
5. Control the mood to suit your approach.
6. Focus on the problem.
7. Establish a time frame for action.
8. Advise of sanctions for inaction.
9. Exert pressure through copy power.

§ 8.05 Proof-Positive Notice

Correspondence provides you with the opportunity to identify yourself, your client, and the capacity in which you are acting. The identification of your client and authority to act on the client's behalf are very important procedural points in certain types of legal disputes.

Consider a standard opening such as: Please be advised that our firm has been retained by Spring Ridge Nursery, Inc., of Houston, Texas, and its president, Mr. J. H. Oakes, has authorized us to contact you regarding....

Often the mere arrival of a demand letter prepared by a lawyer will bring an air of seriousness to a dispute that did not exist before counsel became involved. Most people, including lawyers, become uneasy when they find an unexpected piece of correspondence in their mailbox bearing the return address of a lawyer.

To ensure that your demand letter hits the target, be sure it is sent certified mail, return receipt requested. This prevents the recipient from claiming that she never received your letter. It is also another way to increase the impact of your letter and establish proof-positive notice that the recipient accepted it.

In addition, be sure to designate your demand letter as certified mail, return receipt requested, on the inside address as well as the mailing envelope. By doing so, you will add a sense of formality and urgency to your letter. Consequently, the recipient is likely to be more concerned about its content.

§ 8.06 Educate the Recipient as to the Facts

Correspondence can serve an excellent instructional function in explaining your client's point of view or version of the facts of a particular case without interruption or digression. A well-written demand letter should set forth the basis of your client's claim in a logical and organized manner in language calculated to promote favorable results.

A primary objective of your demand letter should be to convince the other side of the reasonableness and accuracy of the facts presented so as to compel favorable action by the reader. By presenting the facts in a reasonable and evenhanded manner, you will lead the other side to one inescapable conclusion—that he should act in accordance with the request made in the letter.

Several key phrases can help accomplish this objective. For instance, beginning the fact presentation paragraph of your letter with "According to our client . . . " serves to show the other side you recognize that his interpretation of the facts may be different. By acknowledging that the facts presented in your letter represent your client's viewpoint, you promote communication and open exchange with the opposition.

Practice Tip: As any experienced lawyer knows, clients often tell their lawyers what they want the lawyer to know or what they think the lawyer wants to hear. Consequently, it is dangerous to assume you know the whole story after you have heard only one version of the facts. Do not box yourself in by blindly accepting your client's version of the facts. Leave yourself room for maneuvering in case your client's version of the story is not totally accurate. The phrase "according to our client" will help do just that.

To further promote open exchange of communication, prevent misunderstandings, and put your opponent in a position of having to respond, insert the following phrase: "However, if our client is not aware of all the facts surrounding this matter, please advise us accordingly." It helps to follow with, "In the event we do not hear from you on or before (deadline date), we must assume the facts related by our client are accurate and complete."

§ 8.07 Highlight Favorable Facts

One of the advantages of preparing correspondence is that you are in a position to formulate the letter to accent your client's position favorably. If, for instance, the facts tend to lean in your direction, highlight those facts. If, on the other hand, the law is in your favor, talk about the legal aspects of the case. Regardless of your strong point, highlight and magnify them in your demand letter.

§ 8.08 Minimize Damaging Facts

Conversely, correspondence is an excellent way to downplay damaging facts. There is no requirement that you draw attention to or highlight the negative aspects of your client's case. The structure of your letter, word choice, and the presence or omission of certain points can help you devalue and deemphasize the negative aspects of your client's case. Your objective is to convince the opposition that your client has no weak points. Sometimes that objective is best served by simply steering away from disputed facts, if possible.

§ 8.09 Control the Mood to Suit Your Approach

A derivative advantage of highlighting strong points and minimizing weak ones is the ability to control the mood and tone of your approach with the opposition. For example, assume you receive a letter from the other side deriding your client and raising several new issues that you consider to be irrelevant to the case. The tendency is to fire back with a strongly worded rejoinder of your own.

The danger of this approach is an escalation of harsh feelings and polarized positions, or even a break-off of talks. Normally, this is the one consequence you want to avoid. It will usually be in your client's best interest to maintain a dialogue with the other side. You can use correspondence to regulate the tone of your response to accomplish this purpose. For instance, your response could begin with "This will acknowledge and thank you for your letter of...."

From this point on, pick and choose the topics you wish to address in a nonemotional, businesslike manner. The necessary conciliatory mood was created in the first sentence. The remainder of the letter should be drafted to support this tone throughout.

§ 8.10 Focus on the Problem

Always keep correspondence focused on the real problem. Conversely, a good strategy for situations in which the law and facts are both against you is to "muddy the water" or confuse and entangle issues to a point where the real problem becomes camouflaged and sometimes lost. Correspondence can keep you and your opponent on or off track as the situation warrants.

> ***Practice Tip:*** A good time to use correspondence to focus on desired topics is immediately following a meeting or telephone conversation in which a number of unrelated collateral issues may have been injected into the discussion. A letter sent to your opponent immediately after the discussion omitting all the unrelated topics and emphasizing the ones you deem important serves to keep the negotiation focused on the real topics of concern to you.

§ 8.11 Establish a Time Frame for Action

One of the most important aspects of any demand letter is to motivate the other side to take action or refrain from taking action. A principle component in achieving this result is establishing a time frame in which you expect the other side to act. Correspondence is an excellent way of imposing a deadline on an opponent.

When a deadline is imposed orally, there is margin for misinterpretation. However, when the letter imposes the deadline, especially when it is a confirmation of a deadline already imposed in a previous discussion, there is no room for error. Imposing your deadline by letter tends to make the other side accept the time frame as authentic. The permanence of writing also tends to underscore and give added emphasis to the deadline.

§ 8.12 Advise of Sanctions for Inaction

Ignorance is bliss—especially within the context of negotiation. Often when dealing with nonlawyers, unless you state specific sanctions that could be imposed, the opposing party may have no idea of the consequences of inaction. Consequently, it is important for you to educate the opposition as to their potential exposure and liability.

An effective way of making the opposition aware of potential negative repercussions is to suggest the course of action you intend to pursue should the opposition fail to take the action requested in your letter.

For instance, the following phrase could be used: "In the event we do not hear from you on or before the above date, we will have no other alternative but to institute appropriate legal proceedings. If such action becomes necessary, we will request the court to grant us attorney fees, pre- and post-judgment interest, and all costs of court in addition to the principal amount demanded herein."

> ***Practice Tip:*** Once your opponent realizes that failure to meet your demands may result in far greater costs in the future, there is a greater likelihood of compelling him to act in your favor. The key is making your opponent aware of what could happen if he does not meet your demands.

§ 8.13 Exert Pressure Through Copy Power

Demand correspondence should not necessarily be confined just to the sender and the receiver. Involving other parties in the written communication can further strengthen the demand letter. We refer to this ploy as "copy power."

Everyone has a superior or watchdog of some kind. Officers of large public corporations have directors, shareholders, and government regulatory agencies. Employees have employers. Lawyers have their clients, judges, and fellow lawyers. We are all subject to review and reprimand. Consequently, we all have certain pressure points. You can create leverage by exploiting the opposition's pressure points through copy power.

Practice Tip: Copy power is particularly effective when dealing with large organizations and governmental entities. If you want to substantially increase your chances of getting a large corporation or federal agency to act, send a copy of your demand letter to appropriate corporate officials or elected officers. More times than not you will provoke a response or reaction that will help you achieve the desired result.

Despite the pros of copy power, there are downside risks as well. There is always the possibility of backing your opponent into a corner or alienating those you seek to influence with a copy of your letter. Always think twice before invoking copy power.

§ 8.14 Gaining the Edge in Paperwork

All of the points covered in this discussion of demand letters apply equally to other forms of correspondence used in negotiation. Letters, memoranda, e-mails, and draft agreements can be used for much more than just basic communication. Each of the nine points listed above can be used separately or in conjunction with each other to give you an edge in your paperwork.

§ 8.15 Instant Communication Requires That You Think Before You Write Or Talk

Because so much can be accomplished in written communications or phone conversation, we urge you to subscribe to this basic rule: Think before you write or talk. This admonition has never been more important than it is today when just about everyone has a Blackberry or iPhone that allows instant access to almost anywhere in the world. Just because it is easy and convenient to communicate anywhere and at any time, doesn't mean you should.

The predigital days of snail mail and rotary phones imposed a certain restraint on attorneys, requiring them to make decisions more deliberately. Today it is just the opposite. The ease of sending an e-mail or using a cell phone to make a call can easily cloud an attorney's judgment, causing her to act impulsively. We have all had the experience of sending or receiving an ill-conceived e-mail that should have been more carefully considered. While the communication might have been instantaneous, the message too often is not in the best interests of the sender or his clients.

9
Counterattacking

Many experienced lawyers will tell you that the best defense is a good offense. They are right. Why? Because the key to fending off threats of a lawsuit and shifting the momentum of bargaining in your favor is putting your opponent "at risk."

§ 9.01 The "At Risk" Factor Underlies All Effective Counterattacks

The movie "Ransom," starring Mel Gibson, has a dramatic scene that demonstrates the "at-risk" ploy. Gibson plays a wealthy airline executive whose seven-year-old son is kidnapped. In an attempt to communicate with the kidnappers, he appears on television, ostensibly to beg for his son's safety and to display the ransom money demanded by the kidnappers. But instead of pleading for his son's life, as everyone assumes he's going to do, he goes on the offensive. He announces that the ransom money he displays is not to pay the kidnappers. Rather, it is to pay the informants who turn in the kidnappers. At that moment, Gibson goes from the hunted to the hunter by putting the abductors at risk.

Every lawyer has been in the position of representing an angry client who wanted to sue someone regardless of the chances of recovery. Typically, the case is reviewed and an opinion rendered regarding the feasibility of obtaining a judgment. Even though the outlook is not bright, there are always clients who want the suit filed anyway. However, if the client is alerted to possible counterclaim exposure, the case suddenly takes on a different complexion. The enraged client becomes more subdued and starts analyzing his alternatives in a more rational manner. In many cases, the client is willing to forget about a lawsuit that might expose him to liability. This is the "at risk" concept in action.

People are motivated by self-interest. They institute lawsuits only when they believe their self-interest will be served. However, when self-interest is placed in jeopardy, or at risk, potential plaintiffs become hesitant about resorting to litigation. This is true, even in situations in which their claims may be meritorious and have a good chance of success. Suing is one thing; being sued is quite another. The effectiveness of all of the counterattacking ploys described in this chapter hinge on your ability to find ways to put your opponent at risk.

§ 9.02 Counterdemands: How They Work

Everyone is subject to demands. A quick way to reverse the demand pattern is to issue demands of your own. To illustrate the use of counterdemands, consider the following domestic relations case.

The husband's lawyer has tactfully persuaded opposing counsel to make the first settlement proposal. Instead of coming forward with a reasonable offer upon which future discussions can proceed, the wife shoots for the moon. She wants everything and nothing less. The husband's lawyer must respond to her preposterous demands. How should he approach his opponent? Should he counter with a reasonable demand, or try to explain why the wife's demands are too high?

The husband's lawyer does neither. Instead, he makes a counterdemand that is an exact duplicate of the wife's demand, the only difference being that it is the husband who is shooting for the moon. The counterdemand cancels the wife's demand; the case goes back to square one. The wife and her lawyer are again put in the situation of having to make a realistic proposal or letting the status quo remain unchanged. The only other alternative is to accept the husband's demand or use it as a basis for negotiation.

Once in a while, an inexperienced negotiator will fall into the trap of giving credence to an outrageous offer while abandoning his own exorbitant demands. This does not occur often, but it has happened.

§ 9.03 Fighting Fire with Fire

In the previous example, the husband's lawyer countered his opponent's demand by matching it with one equally unworthy of consideration. In this context, counterdemands say to an opponent, "If you have the gall to think I'll consider such a ridiculous demand, then I have the gall to ask you to consider the same terms." The lesson is clear. When you are presented with a situation in which a totally unrealistic demand is being made of you, neutralize it with a corresponding counterdemand. Fight fire with fire.

Practice Tip: Most demands made by your opponents will not be completely out of line. Nonetheless, even when confronted with a realistic demand, a counterdemand of your own will put your opponent at risk.

---

§ 9.04 Concessions Make the Negotiation Process Work

In the real world of negotiation, sooner or later everyone will be in the undesirable position of having to make concessions. No one likes to make concessions; nonetheless, experienced negotiators know that they are necessary to resolve disputes and reach consensus. In short, no one wins every issue every time. In fact, concessions, along with leverage, are at the heart of the bargaining process. Without concessions, there would be no compromise and very few agreements struck. The sooner this fundamental truth is acknowledged, the easier it is to focus on making the right kind of concessions rather than trying to avoid making any concessions at all.

Unfortunately, many less experienced or shortsighted negotiators fail to appreciate the positive role concessions play in the overall process. They view concessions made by opponents as a sign of weakness. To these negotiators, a concession is a red flag that spurs them to demand more and concede less. The result is an ever-increasing list of demands fueled by additional concessions. This creates a vicious cycle of escalation that usually results in collapsed talks and no agreement. Pushing an opponent too far, asking for too much, or making too many demands are characteristic of an overreaching bargainer who just cannot seem to understand why she is not more effective.

Of course, the astute negotiator will soon realize this flaw and take steps to exploit the inherent dangers of overreaching. One way to do this is by using the "vanishing concession."

§ 9.05 The Vanishing Concession: An Effective Way to Counteract Overreaching

The vanishing concession is based on the premise that, once a concession is extracted from an opponent, harmful consequences will result if that concession must be relinquished. The negative consequences can be psychological as well as monetary. The client tends to view the damage in monetary terms. For the lawyer-negotiator, relinquishing the spoils of victory is more damaging from a psychological standpoint. In some instances, the client's confidence in her lawyer can be undermined if the lawyer is forced to give up what the client thought had been won. These effects often provide the impetus to break the cycle of overreaching and shift the momentum of bargaining to the negotiator using this counterattacking ploy. To understand the vanishing concession fully, consider the following example.

§ 9.06 The Withdrawn Offer

Jimmy Powell is a 58-year-old insurance adjuster who has worked in the claims department of a major insurance company for over 30 years. Dale Eager, a young plaintiff's lawyer, has recently notified Jimmy of a claim against the insurance company for injuries sustained by his client, Judy Spender. The insurance company has admitted responsibility for the liability of its insured. The only question is how much it will pay Dale's client.

During the early stages of the negotiation, the parties jockey for position by making extreme offers and counteroffers designed to narrow the true settlement limits. Jimmy refuses to offer more than $2,000 while Dale remains steadfast in his demand for $35,000. Confidentially, Dale believes his case has a realistic settlement value of $10,000 to $12,000.

After the usual pattern of opening moves between the negotiators, Dale decides to accelerate the bargaining process and sends Jimmy a copy of the complaint he intends to file if the matter cannot be settled in the near future. Shortly thereafter, Jimmy announces that he is ready to get down to serious business and wishes to dispose of the case by settlement.

In this spirit of fairness and cooperation, Jimmy offers Dale $7,500. Dale considers the offer a major concession since the highest offer previously made by the insurance company was only $2,000. Elated by this fortunate turn of events, Dale informs his client of the insurance company's offer. Judy is also pleased with the offer and with Dale's obvious negotiation skills. Judy feels good about having retained Dale even though several of her friends recommended that she retain Tom Cook, an older, more experienced lawyer, to handle her case. Dale asks Judy to think about the offer for a few days before he responds to the insurance company.

Judy joyfully starts calculating what portion of the $7,500 settlement will be hers and, just for fun, fantasizes about how she would spend it. After engaging in her imaginary shopping spree, Judy concludes that her portion of the settlement is not enough to cover her inflated financial needs. Consequently, she advises Dale to try to get $10,000 instead of $7,500 from the insurance company.

Spurred on by the insurance company's major concession, Dale tells Judy he is confident he can squeeze another $2,000 or $3,000 out of Jimmy. Dale informs Jimmy that Judy wishes to decline the $7,500 offer but that she would be willing to accept $15,000. By making a demand for $15,000, Dale assumes Jimmy will counter with $8,500. In Dale's view, the ensuing pattern of haggling should result in an agreement somewhere in the $10,000 range.

Instead of engaging in Dale's calculated game of give and take, Jimmy does not make a counteroffer. Jimmy advises Dale that his regional supervisor has reviewed the file and believes that $7,500 is too much to pay for a settlement in this case. Jimmy tells Dale that he is under direct orders to withdraw the $7,500 offer—unless, of course, it is accepted prior to notification of its withdrawal. Since Jimmy is due to report back to his superior by the end of the day, he agrees to give Dale the rest of the day to make a decision. Jimmy's final words are, "It's up to you, Dale. If your client wants the $7,500 settlement, fine. I'll tell my supervisor you accepted the company's offer before I withdrew it. If you don't want to settle today for $7,500, then consider the offer withdrawn. That's the best I can do."

To make matters worse, Judy had miscalculated her portion of the $7,500 settlement and has been trying to contact Dale to press for even more than the $10,000 they had discussed. She is confident Dale will have no trouble getting it. What Dale thought he had won suddenly begins to dissolve. Jimmy turned the tables on Dale and Judy with the vanishing concession.

§ 9.07 The Threat of Bankruptcy

The principle behind the vanishing concession is frequently used in debtor-creditor negotiations in which the debtor is attempting to settle an outstanding account with the creditor at a reduced amount in an effort to avoid bankruptcy. If the creditor is adamant and unwilling to agree to some type of realistic liquidation plan, the debtor invokes a modified version of the vanishing concession ploy. The exchange usually goes something like this:

Creditor's Lawyer: "I'm sorry, but my client is unable to accept your settlement proposal of $5,200. Unless full payment is made, I've been instructed to file suit."

Debtor's Lawyer: "Well, that's a shame, I was hoping we could avoid such drastic action. My client's in a situation where he must either get help from his creditors or be forced to file a petition with the bankruptcy court. He would like to save everyone from suffering a complete loss on their accounts, but he can't do it without some cooperation."

Assuming that bankruptcy would, in fact, diminish the creditor's chance of recovery, the $5,200 offer starts looking a little better, especially when it starts dissolving. The creditor's lawyer knows that if he pushes too hard, the $5,200 may vanish completely.

PRACTICE TIP: Once a concession has been gained, especially if the negotiator and his client have had to invest substantial amounts of time and resources to get it, the prospect of giving it back can be extremely damaging to the apparent victor; therein lies the strength of the vanishing concession.

---

§ 9.08 Substituting New Players to Get Stalled Negotiations Moving Again

From a counterattacking standpoint, limited authority provides you with the ability to change participants whenever the situation dictates. Playing this negotiating card can be valuable when talks have reached a stalemate and breakdown is imminent. Negotiating from an announced position of limited authority gives you the opportunity to substitute participants when the need arises. The ploy of changing participants is illustrated in the following example.

§ 9.09 How Substituting New Players Can Avoid Catastrophe

Assume you are engaged in a negotiation with a large bank on behalf of your client, Paul Welch. Your objective is to keep the bank from foreclosing on Paul's property and to convince the bank's representative that it would be mutually beneficial to reschedule all of Paul's loans at a lower interest rate over an extended payout period. Throughout the negotiation, you inform the bank's representative, F.M. Bancshares, that if the bank will agree to your plan, Paul's millionaire father-in-law will voluntarily make a sizable payment to reduce the principal balance.

F.M.'s position is inflexible—bring the loans current or else. Eventually talks break down. F.M. informs you that the bank will start foreclosure proceedings at the end of the week. You decide to do two things: first, substitute negotiators; second, appeal to a higher authority. You convince Paul's father-in-law, who is eager to help, to contact the bank's president for an appointment to discuss Paul's problem. The bank's president is receptive to keeping the talks open, since it appears that F.M.'s hard-line attitude may have alienated Paul and his father-in-law. The president knows that, unless Paul's father-in-law steps in to help, the bank will have to foreclose on the property and will be faced with a sizable loss.

Since Paul has pledged his business assets as collateral for the loan, foreclosure would effectively put him out of business, drying up his only source of income. Paul would have only one alternative at that point—bankruptcy. However, the introduction of new participants can help break the impasse, enabling the negotiation to continue. The prospect of financial loss for all the parties is substantially lessened.

In the foregoing example, the first set of negotiators could not resolve the problem. Without a new twist, the negotiation would have ended in stalemate, forcing the bank to make its only remaining move—foreclosure. The talks were given new life by substituting new participants, who continued the negotiation process with a higher level of decision-making authority and without the past rancor that had characterized the bargaining between the lawyer and bank officer. What seemed like a hopeless situation was transformed into a new negotiation.

§ 9.10 The Ultimate Threat: What to Do When All Else Fails

Another effective counterattacking ploy is to make the ultimate threat. When all else has failed and you elect to invoke your ultimate threat, you put your opponent in the maximum at-risk situation. This ploy can be delivered in the following three ways.

§ 9.11 Raising the Stakes

When an impasse has been reached and you have decided you must bring the negotiation to a conclusion, raise the stakes to such a point that your opponent cannot stay in the game. For instance, in a hard-fought lawsuit that rests on highly technical points of law, inform your opponent that you have decided to employ additional expert witnesses. If the opposition is not in a position to match you dollar for dollar and hour for hour in responding to your new experts, you may force a settlement on favorable terms because the stakes have become too great for your opponent to stay in the game.

§ 9.12 The Ultimatum

Typically, this ploy is used in collective-bargaining talks. Labor's ultimate threat is to call a strike. The ultimatum can be a very powerful ploy once it is established as being credible and potentially damaging. It creates pressure that can break a logjam caused by management's reticence. Ultimatums are frequently made in legal negotiations. Aside from labor negotiations, the most common is the threat of suit: "Either pay my client or we'll file suit."

§ 9.13 Withdrawal

Another ultimate threat counterattacking ploy is withdrawal. This ploy is frequently used in diplomatic negotiations. The object of withdrawal is to put the opposition at risk by threatening to break off negotiations. This ploy is most effective when the status quo is in your favor.

For example, assume a superstar professional athlete has issued an ultimatum to his team demanding a substantial pay increase. The team's owner calls the superstar's bluff by refusing to meet his salary demands. By doing so, the owner has taken a calculated risk: Drop your demands or walk. The athlete chooses the latter course of action. He walks right into the inviting alternative of a lucrative motion-picture career. Subsequently, talks resume. At this point the athlete is in a perfect position to put the team's owner at risk by threatening to break off the negotiation. The player's downside risks are minimal because of the alternative of a movie career. The newly created status quo suits him fine.

The burden now shifts to the owner. The player's demands are no longer backed by bluffs or empty threats. It will be up to the owner to reverse the new status quo. The threat of withdrawal makes the player's demands seem a great deal more palatable to the club owner.

§ 9.14 Fighting Back: Counterclaims, Crossclaims, and Third-Party Actions

Trial lawyers are well aware of the power of counterclaims, crossclaims, and third-party actions. In defense litigation, fighting back is often the most effective at-risk device available to the lawyer. If you want to counterattack in the world of litigation, you counterclaim, crossclaim, or institute a third-party action. Consider the following example.

§ 9.15 The Story of Dr. Allen

Dr. Frank Allen is a world-renowned petroleum geologist. Early in his career, he worked for a small oil company organized in a foreign tax haven. After six years of productive work for the company and after investing a substantial amount of his own money in the company, he decided to embark on a career as an independent petroleum geologist.

Once he had begun building his own company, it became apparent that the minority interest he had acquired in his former company was worth little to him. Management in his old firm simply ignored Dr. Allen. He was not reelected to serve as a director, nor was he given notice of any shareholder meetings or afforded the right to participate in the company's shareholder stock option programs.

To make matters worse, the company's profit-and-loss position was marginal and deteriorating fast. There was little money for exploration and expansion. As far as Dr. Allen was concerned, his former company's future was bleak. Some months after Dr. Allen had resigned himself to this reality, word reached him that his former company had discovered one of the largest oil fields in the Indian Ocean. Not surprisingly, the entire project had been conceived by Dr. Allen from its inception. The discovery completely changed the company's financial outlook. The marginal balance sheet was replaced by one of unlimited potential.

Despite the role Dr. Allen played in helping the company find such a bonanza, he was still being squeezed out. He was a minority stockholder with little or no influence. Dr. Allen made attempts to sell his stock but, because the company was closely held, there were few bona fide prospects. Finally, after several months, a representative of an investment group expressing interest in acquiring his shares (if the price was right) contacted him. Eager to sell, Dr. Allen entered into negotiations with the investment group without the aid of legal counsel.

Within a very short time, a deal was made whereby Dr. Allen agreed to sell all his shares to the investment group for $1 million. The parties exchanged correspondence and the investment group's lawyer sent Dr. Allen a confirmation letter. The deal was locked up and set for closing in 14 days. Dr. Allen was pleased that at long last he would finally reap the rewards of his labor and financial investment.

Three days before the actual exchange of stock and money was to take place, an international business newspaper published a story announcing that Dr. Allen's former company was going to be acquired by another company on a one-for-one stock exchange. The acquiring company's stock, which was publicly traded, was trading for $100 per share. What Dr. Allen had sold for $1 million was going to be worth $10 million after the acquisition. Dr. Allen was sick, but what could he do? He had exchanged documents and approved the trade by a confirmation letter. The deal appeared to be airtight.

When Dr. Allen voiced his reluctance about carrying out the trade, he was quickly told by the investment group's lawyer, "We have a deal. Tender your shares or we'll file suit." Ultimately, the investment group filed suit against Dr. Allen when he refused to conclude the sale.

The lawyers defending Dr. Allen were quick to recognize his dilemma. He had been a victim of insider trading. It appeared that two members of the purchasing investment group were also close friends of one of the directors of Dr. Allen's former company. The main problem was finding a connection between the parties in an attempt to counter the correspondence and the confirmation letter that Dr. Allen signed.

Realizing that the transaction was probably originated by the inside director, Dr. Allen's lawyers decided to put the investment group at risk by bringing an action against the two members of the investment group for alleged insider trading. In addition, a third-party action was brought against all of the directors of his former company for failure to notify Dr. Allen of the pending acquisition. In the event the court compelled Dr. Allen to tender his shares to the purchaser for $1 million, his suit would seek recovery of his lost profit from the directors of his former company. The inside traders were faced with the possibility of losing everything they might gain if the case against Dr. Allen prevailed. In the end, the suit against Dr. Allen was dropped, thereby freeing him to trade his shares for their full $10 million value. The counteractions used by Dr. Allen's lawyer put the opposition at risk to the point of saving Dr. Allen $9 million.

Practice Tip: When involved as a defendant in litigation, find a way to put the plaintiff at risk by counterattacking. Depending on the facts of the case, counterclaims, cross-claims, and third-party actions will often provide you the ammunition you need to put the opposition at risk.

§ 9.16 The Affirmative Defense

As plaintiff's lawyers will attest, the affirmative defense is second only to a counterclaim in terms of counterattacking effectiveness. The only thing better than a strong affirmative defense is two, three, or more strong affirmative defenses. They make the case more complicated for the plaintiff to prove. A complicated case becomes harder to win because of the increased number of barriers and potential pitfalls produced by the affirmative defenses. Multiple affirmative defenses make the case harder to explain to a judge or jury.

§ 9.17 Creating Patterned Disorder

In those situations where the counterclaim alternative is not available, you can use another counterattacking ploy—creating patterned disorder. Consider the following example.

§ 9.18 The Disorganized Businessman

Sam Krotek is a successful businessman. Unfortunately, however, he is involved in too many projects. As a result of Sam's aggressiveness, his organization is in a constant state of disarray. His business records and organizational structure are in a mess, at least in the opinions of his lawyer and accountant. Despite this, Sam has no trouble finding what he wants to find. The fact is, Sam knows where everything is, and exactly how to retrieve it.

When Sam's lawyer advises him to clean up his mess, he just laughs. "Why destroy my fortress? I'm safe inside my disorganization. If my own lawyer can't untangle this mess, how can you expect the Internal Revenue Service or some plaintiff's lawyer to do it?"

Sam's attitude may not be prudent for many reasons. However, the truth is, he is right about cloaking himself in disorder. As long as you know the secret to untangling the mess if and when necessary, patterned disorder can be useful as a counterattacking ploy. In essence, it tells the opposition, "Catch me if you can find me." Uncertainties associated with the disorganization put the opposition at risk.

§ 9.19 Patterned Disorder: Turning a Disadvantage into an Advantage

Patterned disorder raises barriers against anyone trying to assault you. While we certainly do not recommend that people consciously create a tangle of disorder, disorder can be a disadvantage that becomes an advantage. Conversely, be aware that patterned disorder can be used effectively against you if you ever have occasion to unsnarl the records of a party defendant who owns controlling interest in more paper corporations and marginal bank accounts than any three Fortune 500 companies combined.

10
Fallback Strategy: A Systematic Approach to Dealing with Setbacks

Lawyers are pessimists by nature. While they may hope for the best, they plan for the worst. A lawyer's legal training and experience is geared toward anticipating potential problems. This is why lawyers are better equipped than most to handle the inevitable setbacks that are bound to occur over the course of a typical negotiation. Awareness of proven principles and techniques for dealing with the worst if and when it comes is the best insurance any negotiator can have against disaster. This chapter provides a systematic approach to making the best of a bad situation.

§ 10.01 The Fatal Assumption That Negotiation Must Result in Agreement

The worst mistake any negotiator can make is to assume that a negotiation must result in an agreement in order to be successful. People have been dealing themselves undue misery and disappointment for centuries because of their steadfast devotion to this erroneous assumption. Victims of this fatal assumption equate a successful negotiation with reaching an agreement, any agreement, merely for the sake of saying, "but at least we closed the deal."

Members of the "agreement at all costs" club tend to lose sight of just why they are negotiating in the first place. At the outset of the negotiation, the purpose is clear: You negotiate to improve the status quo. However, once the ultimate goal shifts to merely reaching an agreement for the sake of an agreement, substantive negotiating objectives will likely take a back seat to the new priority of closing the deal. When this happens, the seeds of disaster are sown.

Overcoming the deeply ingrained notion that a negotiation must produce an agreement is the key to developing an effective fallback strategy. Recognizing that your success does not necessarily ride on your ability to forge some type of agreement will provide you with an instant and significant advantage over your opponents, especially those who remain committed to an agreement at all costs.

Refusing to be constrained by having to make a deal allows you to be bolder and more confident in your conduct in a given negotiation. This approach also forces you to come to grips with your alternatives. By doing this, you will have effectively constructed a safety net under the negotiation to cushion the blow of failing to reach agreement. That same safety net is not available to the opponent who sees no alternative to reaching a negotiated agreement.

§ 10.02 Assuming That You Must Act

Another common, erroneous assumption is that you must act, even if action is likely to be futile. How many times have you heard "I have to do something, even if it is wrong" uttered in crisis situations? Probably all too often, even in spite of the futility of such action.

This is not to suggest that freezing up and doing nothing is the best way to confront a crisis. When you are in desperate straits, you indeed "have to do something." But how logical is it to take action you know will prove ineffective or even counterproductive? This seemingly obvious bit of common sense should be considered in every crisis negotiation. Unfortunately, it is not.

PRACTICE TIP: Whenever you are convinced that a negotiated agreement cannot or will not accomplish your objectives, you should admit that you are wasting your time. This is your cue to seek an alternative solution. Even if none is readily available, it does not make sense to seek an agreement that will leave you in worse shape. You would be much better advised to work in the garden or play golf. At least you would have the comfort of knowing you were not actively making things any worse. In most cases, the status quo can hold its own without you.

---

§ 10.03 BATNA: The Centerpiece of a Strategic Walk-Away Position

As you recall, we urged you to adopt Roger Fisher and William Ury's concept of BATNA (Best Alternative to a Negotiated Agreement) as the final part of your short-term preparation regimen. While the material in Chapter 4 shows you how to formulate a BATNA position, it does not fully articulate the importance of the concept or the leverage advantages to be derived.

§ 10.04 Capitalizing on the Defensive Leverage Advantages of the Walk-Away Position

Once you have analyzed the situation, identified your alternatives, and formulated your BATNA position, you have created a potentially powerful defensive leverage advantage. By accepting the possibility that the negotiation could fail to achieve your objectives and identifying your alternatives at the outset, you deprive your opponent of much of the effective use of the leverage of uncertainty. You have psychologically insulated yourself from failure. You have also allowed yourself the luxury of making difficult decisions objectively without being subjected to the pressures of a crisis situation.

Consequently, if and when a crisis comes, you will have already developed a well-reasoned alternative course of action. This tends to deprive the opponent of leverage involving sanctions, uncertainty, and the use of deadlines.

§ 10.05 The Walk-Away Position as Leverage in Reserve

The walk-away position is also a powerful offensive leverage device. A credible threat to break off talks and seek alternative courses of action can create a high degree of uncertainty in the mind of your opponent. As a result, communicating your walk-away position can often turn the tables on an opponent and extract concessions neither party thought possible. This equalizing effect has the potential to change the entire character and momentum of a negotiation. This is one more reason why developing a walk-away position should receive high priority in all of your prenegotiation organization and planning.

§ 10.06 Objectivity, Realism, and Flexibility

Developing a workable walk-away position requires an objective and realistic analysis of the circumstances confronting you. Because miscalculation is an ever-present danger, you should strive to avoid the dangers of subjectivity, unfounded optimism, and acting on insufficient information. It is also vitally important to remain flexible and to be willing to adjust your walk-away position as the negotiation unfolds.

It is often helpful to view your walk-away position as you would a share of common stock. The price of the stock fluctuates depending on any number of tangible and intangible factors. The same is true of the walk-away position. For instance, in our personal injury example, failure to locate a key witness, discovery of low insurance limits, or a sudden need for cash by your client can cause you to lower your walk-away position. By the same token, uncovering damaging evidence against the defendant, an ill-advised admission, or an internal deadline working against your opponent can drive up the walk-away position. In either event, failure to adjust your position accordingly can lead to a disastrous result.

§ 10.07 Communicating Your Walk-Away Position

Communicating your walk-away position is using leverage. Actually activating it is abandoning the entire bargaining relationship. This is why you must carefully weigh all of the implications of communicating or activating the walk-away position. The quickest way to lose your credibility is to make a threat you aren't willing or able to back up. Consequently, you should take extreme care not only to calculate your walk away position, but also to communicate it in an informational tone rather than as a threat or ultimatum.

PRACTICE TIP: If and when you do decide to walk away from a negotiation, make sure you are willing and able to move to a workable alternative. Nothing is worse than walking out on a negotiation only to return a day or a week later with hat in hand. You rarely get a second chance under such circumstances.

---

§ 10.08 Mastering the Principles of Contingency Planning

While using the BATNA concept as the centerpiece of developing a strategic walk-away position will undoubtedly confer invaluable offensive and defensive negotiating benefits, it is certainly not the only fallback technique available to you. Short-run or tactical fallback techniques based on the principles of contingency planning should be used to complete your strategic fallback position. Together with your BATNA position, these additional principles and techniques should combine to play an integral role in preparing and executing any negotiation plan.

§ 10.09 Anticipation and Flexibility: The Keys to Contingency Planning

Unfortunately, many overly optimistic negotiators overlook the reality that things do not ever go their way 100 percent of the time. Consequently, they fail to formulate contingency plans to deal with setbacks that are almost sure to occur. When problems do occur, the negotiator is unprepared to deal with them effectively. Decisions aimed at coping with reversals and setbacks are often made under extreme pressure. Because of the crisis atmosphere, available options and alternative courses of action are often ill-defined or overlooked. The consequence is a reactive approach to tactical decision-making. The results are often predictable and many times disastrous.

Anticipation and flexibility are the two keys to combating problems inherent in crisis decision making. By anticipating the tactical moves and responses your opponent is likely to make, you are in a position to act affirmatively by devising well-thought-out fallback measures of your own. By building flexibility into your negotiating plan, you are able to create effective short-term safety valves and escape hatches to deal with reversals, much the same way that the walk-away position provides a strategic safety net under your long-term negotiating objectives.

§ 10.10 How to Build in a Time Cushion

When planning a time frame for concluding an agreement, operate under the premise that "everything takes more time than you think." You need only look through dates of correspondence relating to past negotiations in some of your old files to confirm the wisdom of this statement. The best way to cope with this eventuality is to build in a time cushion whenever possible. You can do this in a number of ways.

§ 10.11 The Double Deadline: Yours and Theirs

A favorite approach is to build in internal and external deadlines for agreement as a way of creating extra time that is invariably needed in high-stakes, pressurized negotiations. One should never reveal internal deadlines to the opposition. Conversely, always try to anticipate the opposition's external and internal deadlines.

§ 10.12 Avoiding the Last-Minute Crunch

A second approach to building in a time cushion is to be conscious of the leverage of timing regarding deadline pressures and to respond by trying to accelerate the pace of a negotiation. This enables you to avoid or minimize the leverage of timing that could be exerted against you and your client.

§ 10.13 Planning Alternative Courses of Action

A third technique for building in extra time is to identify alternatives, consider different courses of action, and anticipate actions and possible reactions of your opponents in advance. This tends to insulate you from the dangers of formulating positions and selecting alternatives under unfavorable conditions. This approach makes maximum productive use of your time and avoids the tendency to make concessions in crisis situations.

§ 10.14 Develop Short-Term Fallback Positions

In addition to the foregoing measures, you should constantly be developing short-term fallback positions as the negotiation unfolds. This requires applying the same principles that govern formulation of the walk-away position. The only difference is that short-term fallback planning involves anticipating an opponent's moves at each stage of the bargaining with a corresponding alternative response.

§ 10.15 Asking and Getting

For instance, assume you are attempting to sell a parcel of land. After many offers and counteroffers, you and the lawyer for the potential buyer are still $2,000 apart. At this point, you decide to make a final offer. Because you are so close in price, you know you will not invoke your walk-away position. Nevertheless, you would like to close the price differential as much as possible. Based on the negotiations, you know that if you offered to reduce the price by $1,500, the buyer would almost surely increase his offer by $500. Consequently, this should represent your ultimate short-term fallback.

Confident that you could conclude the agreement on this basis, you decide to reduce your price by $500 on the chance that the prospective buyer might accept it or, alternatively, make a counterproposal to split the difference by upping his offer by $1,000 if you drop the asking price by $1,000. Should both of these approaches fail, you know what your ultimate fallback would be to ensure a deal without an undue delay of time.

PRACTICE TIP: This very basic principle is just one more application of contingency planning. Those negotiators who take the extra time to plan for inevitable long- and short-term setbacks will find themselves in a position of control even when things are not going exactly according to plan. Anticipating problems and formulating contingent responses is the best way to head off a crisis and insulate yourself from the pressures that result when you are confronted by a setback.

§ 10.16 What to Do in a Bad Situation

All the contingency planning and positive thinking in the world cannot help you in situations in which you are outgunned at every turn. Every lawyer has experienced that feeling of helplessness when confronted by an opponent armed with superior leverage, favorable law and facts, numerous alternatives to a negotiated agreement, and all the time in the world in which to make a decision. There is little you can do to turn the tables on a vastly superior opponent.

On the other hand, just because you are on the ropes does not mean the situation is hopeless. There are techniques and principles that negotiators can use to make the best out of a bad situation. This section is devoted to dealing with those unpleasant and hopefully infrequent situations in which the question is not whether you will win or lose, but rather how bad it is going to be.

§ 10.17 Do Not Make the Situation Worse

Often you are in a difficult situation due to circumstances over which you have no control. Other times, your predicament might be due to poor planning, a tactical mistake, acting on insufficient information, or other reasons related to the conduct of the negotiation.

Regardless of the cause of your problem, you want to ensure that you do not add fuel to the fire or compound your troubles. One sure way to make the situation worse is to fall victim to the pressure generated by earlier reversals. Advice not to panic is easy to give and tougher to follow; nonetheless, there are techniques that can be used in even the most nightmarish situations.

§ 10.18 Buy Time to Identify Alternatives and Slow Your Opponent's Momentum

One of the best ways to avoid getting into deeper trouble is to buy time to identify alternatives and analyze the consequences of your actions as well as those of your opponent. Additionally, buying time can often help slow or even halt the other side's momentum. In some cases, circumstances may change with time. In others, you may be only staving off the inevitable, but at least you will be able to prepare for it or possibly work out more advantageous concession terms.

§ 10.19 Do Not Play to Your Opponent's Strengths

When you are finally forced to negotiate under adverse circumstances, you should make every effort to avoid your opponent's strengths. If you are representing a defendant in a personal injury suit involving clear-cut liability and uncertain damages, talk about damages. Point out to your opponent that proving liability will do his client little good if there are no damages.

If the legal precedent supporting your case is weak, argue the facts. If your opponent enjoys superior facts and substantive law, divert the discussion to points of procedure. This is just another way to offset the other party's momentum and delay the final outcome. On occasion, you can divert the direction of the entire negotiation to the point where the original focus is either lost altogether or the opponent's position and leverage are made to appear less persuasive or powerful than they really are.

§ 10.20 Invoke Uncertainty

Even when you are on the ropes, the aggressor is subject to the leverage of uncertainty. Planting a seed of doubt, even if there is little basis for it, can help stem the tide of a negotiation. Leading the other side to believe your position is stronger than it actually is can help stave off defeat.

Practice Tip: This is one of the few situations in which you might want to risk a bluff that you know you cannot back up. If defeat is inevitable, there is probably little to lose and a great deal to gain.

§ 10.21 Play the Walk-Away Card

As discussed above, the ultimate fallback is to play your walk-away card. Unfortunately, this is not always a viable alternative. However, when faced with the choice of reaching an agreement with the devil or walking away into the deep blue sea, a swim may be in order.

§ 10.22 Concession Behavior: The Best Way to Lose

No lawyer is invincible. For whatever the reason, every lawyer has occasionally found herself on the short end of a negotiation. However, even when defeat is inevitable, something can always be done to improve your position. There is a best way to lose based on concession behavior principles and techniques that you can employ immediately. Hopefully, you will not have to resort to these tactics anytime soon, but when a bad day at the bargaining table rolls around, and it will, you will be ready to salvage something for yourself and your client. While it is not your first or even second choice, a qualified surrender beats an unconditional surrender every time.

§ 10.23 Get Something in Return for Your Concession

Always remember that a negotiation is never over until the ink is dry on the agreement. If you must yield to your opponent's demands, try to extract something in return. For example, if you represent a client who owes $40,000 on a secured note and you are forced to pay back the full amount to avoid foreclosure, options are still available to you.

One approach is to admit liability and offer to "work with the bank to ensure full satisfaction of the debt." This might take the form of negotiating installment payments, receiving a limited extension so that funds may be raised, or renewing the loan if additional collateral can be given.

Surprisingly, once you concede liability, the lender will make concessions of its own. The reason is simple: The bank does not want the collateral if it can get its money. By conceding liability and assuming the role of mediator, the bank has newfound hope that it will eventually get its money, which is all it wanted in the first place.

There are other ways to get something of value for your concession. Consider the termination of a commercial contract. If all else fails and you are unable to talk the other side out of exercising its right to terminate, you may want to take the following approach: "Well, Bill, I'm really sorry your client feels that he has to terminate. Losing this order will really hurt my client. Tell you what, it sure would cushion the blow if you could help us avoid the adverse publicity by keeping this out of the trade magazines."

This request will cost the disgruntled customer little or nothing, but could be of real benefit to the client in preserving the confidence of other customers. Assuming such a request is handled properly, the chances are good that the victor will accommodate the losing party.

§ 10.24 Contain Your Losses

The preceding example underscores another crucial point: If you have to lose, contain your losses as much as possible. In the example, one customer has been lost; however, the quick-thinking lawyer took steps at once to cut the client's loss of other customers. While the lost business hurts, the potential adverse publicity could have been disastrous.

§ 10.25 Do Not Concede Everything at Once

When things really look bleak, there is a tendency to become frustrated and overreact. Sometimes total surrender is justified, sometimes it is not. The best approach is to concede one point at a time, starting with the least important and moving to the most important. As a result, the other party may cease its demands short of taking everything for a variety of reasons. Sympathy is one. A perception that the well is dry when it is not is another.

§ 10.26 Concede a Secondary Point to Save a Deal Point

A variation of sequential concessions is making a partial concession look like a total victory for the opposition. This involves conceding a valuable secondary point in exchange for an agreement. Depending on the value of the secondary point, the agreement appears to be a total victory for the other side. In fact, however, the final agreement provides for attaining some less obvious, albeit important objectives for your client. Only you will know what and how much to give up, but in appropriate circumstances it can be a last gasp technique to avert failure.

§ 10.27 Inflate the Worth of the Concession

If you must concede an important point to get an agreement, the circumstances might call for you to inflate the value of the concession to the other party as a way of foregoing continued bargaining that could reveal other weaknesses in your position. This technique is also helpful in extracting something of value in return for your concession.

§ 10.28 Mask the Damage

Conversely, the circumstances may require that you mask the damage caused by your concessions or minimize the importance it has on your client. This is true in situations where the true extent of the damage done could reveal other weaknesses in your position or undermine your client's long-term objectives. Examples include revelations that could erode public confidence in your client, disclosure of cash-flow problems, or revelation of other internal problems.

§ 10.29 Keep Your Client Informed

From the client's standpoint, the best way to emerge relatively intact from a losing situation is to keep the client informed every step of the way. Surveys indicate that client satisfaction has little to do with the results their lawyers are able to accomplish for them. Rather, it is the lawyer's attitude toward the client and his problem and the lawyer's willingness to keep the client apprised of the situation that count most. This is why you should consult your client every step of the way. Document the negotiation's progress or lack of it with phone calls, letters, and meetings. Always present your client with a realistic picture of what is happening and what is likely to happen, as well as available alternatives.

Finally, be honest about where the client stands and what his chances are. If the situation looks bad, you should prepare your client for the worst. Conversely, if the situation initially looks good, you should still prepare your client for the worst. Things change, and when they do, no surprise is a good surprise.

§ 10.30 Keep It Professional

Finally, you should always face defeat as professionally as you accept victory. Yelling, swearing, or crying will not do you a lot of good at this point. Remember, there will be other battles, often with the same players. When that happens, you will be remembered not so much for winning or losing, but for how you handled it. Just because you lost a round does not mean you have to forfeit your reputation. Keeping things professional will ensure that you do not.

11
Closing

The outcome of months of investigation, meetings, phone calls, letters, and document drafts can hinge on what is done or said over the span of only a few minutes. At this point, the only thing that counts is the ability to get the other side to say the magic word: Yes. All that has gone on before adds up to zero if the parties are unable to pin down a final, binding agreement. Every lawyer has at least one sad story about the big one that got away. In many of these situations, the deal was lost because of an inability to close.

Because closing is so dependent on one's sense of judgment and timing, and because every negotiation differs in terms of issues, parties, and leverage, it is very difficult to lay down hard-and-fast rules. However, we can point out the factors present in every closing and suggest some basic approaches and techniques aimed at making you more effective in the clutch.

§ 11.01 The Right Time to Close a Negotiation

The right time to close a negotiation is when everyone is ready, willing, and able to say yes to all of the terms embodied in a proposed agreement. Conversely, the wrong time is any other time. The problem lies in pinpointing the right time to close. Your sense of timing and judgment become critical in making this determination.

§ 11.02 Deadlines Can Dictate the Right Time for Closing

In certain negotiations, internal or external deadlines will dictate the right time to close a negotiation. For instance, in a collective bargaining negotiation in which the alternative to an agreement is a strike, the external deadline for closing is almost always the expiration of the contract term then in existence. In other situations, such as where one of the parties is seeking to take advantage of certain tax considerations, the internal deadline for agreement would be just prior to the end of the party's fiscal year for tax purposes.

Where a deadline for agreement is a factor, identifying the appropriate time for closing is a relatively simple matter. Once the deadline is identified, the rest will become fairly obvious. For instance, in the example of the party operating under an internal deadline to take advantage of certain tax deductions, the correct approach would be to use delay tactics to extend the time for closing rather than agree to an earlier closing date the other party will doubtlessly be seeking. In this case, your final offer should coincide with the other party's internal deadline. When the opposition is faced with the choice of making certain concessions to guarantee an agreement versus the risk of reaching no agreement and thus losing all tax benefits, he will most likely make the concessions to close the deal.

§ 11.03 Pushing the Transaction to a Conclusion

Negotiations in which there is little or no deadline pressure to close can prove more difficult. In this type of case, it will be up to one or both of the parties to determine the appropriate time to conclude the agreement. Usually, the party with the superior leverage will be in the best position to specify the time for closing. However, awareness of the time for closing can be used to offset this advantage.

To illustrate, assume a buyer and seller are negotiating the purchase and sale of a certain parcel of commercial real estate. The particular parcel is not a prime piece of land in terms of location. The prospective purchaser is considering several sites. The seller has no other prospective buyers. The original asking price is $200,000 with a 20 percent down payment. The parties are in basic agreement as to all terms except price and financing. The buyer wants to pay less than $200,000, with the cheapest possible financing.

While neither party is in any particular hurry, the seller knows that continued negotiation will serve no purpose other than to provide the prospective buyer more time in which to find a significantly better alternative in terms of price and interest rate. The buyer and seller both have reason to believe that mortgage interest rates will probably drop gradually in the coming months.

Based on these facts, the seller knows that the buyer has little to gain by closing a deal now. He also knows that his chances to make a deal will diminish with time. As a result, the seller decides to take a calculated risk to push for a deal. He decides to tell the prospective buyer that, for personal reasons, he has to make a deal by the end of the week or be forced to withdraw the property from the market. Knowing that this will probably not be enough to ensure a deal, he offers to reduce the price by $5,000 and the down payment by 5 percent and to agree that the first payment will be due in six months to allow the buyer to finance the deal at a possible lower rate of interest.

This action on the part of the seller now requires either a response or a counteroffer from the buyer. In lieu of a positive response, the seller must be prepared to take the property off the market and lose a potential sale, at least for the time being.

§ 11.04 The Buyer's Possible Responses

Let us analyze the buyer's possible responses. A positive response assures a deal. The seller has given up $5,000 on the purchase price, $10,000 in front money, and six months of time before the first payment is due. This illustrates the old adage that 95 percent of something beats 100 percent of nothing every time.

Alternatively the buyer could choose to make a counteroffer. If so, the seller would have the option to close on new terms proposed by the buyer, or answer the counteroffer with a counterproposal of his own in the context of the one-week deadline set earlier by the seller.

If the buyer rejected the seller's proposed terms, the seller would remove the property from the market, at least for the time being. Here the seller has lost little. He can always put the property back on the market within a reasonable period of time. The only thing the seller wants to guard against is a loss of credibility in the eyes of the buyer. When the property does go back on the market, the seller may ultimately reach agreement with this or another buyer. In the meantime, the seller has lost very little since there were no other prospective buyers in the first place.

§ 11.05 The Three Don'ts of Closing

In situations where there is little or no deadline pressure, such as in the previous example, it's up to you to take the initiative in guiding the transaction to a close. In doing so, heed the Three Don'ts of Closing:

1. ***Don't*** press for a closing until you have all the information you need to make an offer or an informed response to an offer.
2. ***Don't*** press for a closing if you feel the other side is not ready to close and would view your efforts with mistrust or suspicion. Being premature or overanxious can deter the other side from making a deal they would otherwise be willing to make.
3. ***Don't*** allow the other side to press for a closing until you are ready to close. Too many negotiators find themselves swept into deals they were not ready to make because they felt pressured.

§ 11.06 Four Proven Closing Techniques

Once you are ready to close but feel the other side is in no hurry, several techniques are available to help guide the negotiation to a conclusion.

§ 11.07 Summarization

This is a time-tested technique in which the party ready to close simply repeats all the elements of the deal in summary form, concluding with phrases such as:

"This is my understanding of the terms. If you are in agreement, I can have the documents prepared." Or:

"Unless you have anything to add, that should wrap it up. So we have a deal!"

Or something else to that effect together with the customary extended hand to seal the agreement with the symbolic handshake.

§ 11.08 Marathon

The "marathon" approach is often used when the parties still have a number of differences. A final meeting is scheduled. After numerous cups of coffee have been consumed, the party seeking to close will finally say something like, "Look, we've been here for hours and at this rate we could be here days from now. We agree on most of the important matters. Let's split the difference on the remaining issues and go home."

Practice Tip: This technique has a better chance of succeeding depending on the lateness of the hour and how close the parties actually are on the major issues.

---

§ 11.09 All or Nothing

This technique involves making a calculated risk to break an impasse and reach an agreement. When there appears to be genuine deadlock, the party seeking to close offers his last trade point or another concession that has been held in reserve. He couples this offer with an announcement that, "This is the very best I can do. As far as I'm concerned, it comes down to this or nothing. Either you meet me halfway or let's just forget everything."

Practice Tip: Of course, there is a risk that the other party will reject the all-or-nothing ultimatum. This is why the all-or-nothing ploy should be a technique of last resort.

§ 11.10 The Multiple-Choice Ploy

Once we were negotiating a settlement agreement on behalf of an entertainer who sued a resort hotel claiming anticipatory repudiation of a performance contract. It was obvious that the hotel would be held liable if the case went to trial. It was also clear that neither the plaintiff nor the defendant wanted a trial. The defense lawyer was dragging his feet in making a final decision settling the case. We surmised that, since the hotel was in a beach resort area, it was probably waiting until the summer months when it would have a better cash flow and could more easily absorb a settlement. It was also obvious that the hotel wanted to forgo any payment for as long as possible.

In order to break the impasse and conclude the agreement, we used the multiple-choice ploy. Our offer included the following alternatives:

1. The plaintiff will accept $15,000 now, or
2. $16,000 within 30 days, or
3. $17,000 within 60 days, or
4. $20,000 spread over six months.

The combination of offering the defendant a delayed payment plan, combined with the power of suggestion, worked. After thinking it over, the hotel chose the third alternative. The case was settled.

§ 11.11 Once Your Opponent Has Agreed to Your Terms - STOP!

Besides never getting around to concluding the deal, the biggest mistake negotiators make in closing is not knowing when to quit. Once the other party has agreed to the deal--STOP! Too many people continue to sell the deal after it has been sold. This tends to have the effect of scaring the other side away, of disclosing information that makes the other side rethink its position, or of reopening topics already agreed on for further negotiation.

The best way to guard against overselling the deal is to shake hands, promise to have the paperwork delivered for signature as soon as possible, and leave. If the transaction is made over the telephone, simply conclude the conversation. This makes it impossible to talk yourself out of what you spent so much time talking yourself into.

§ 11.12 Finish the Paperwork Quickly

Because most agreements involve a written contract or a court or consent order before the transaction is finalized, it is important not to procrastinate on the paperwork. By the same token, do not let the other side cause problems because of their own delay. The best way to take care of this is to (1) volunteer to do the drafting, and (2) make the drafting your top priority.

> ***PRACTICE TIP:*** If the other side insists on doing the drafting, do not hesitate to prod them. Create a sense of urgency or use a deadline such as a business trip or court appearance to spur the other side to take action.

§ 11.13 The Secondary Negotiation

The transaction is never concluded until the papers are signed. More than one handshake deal has fallen apart because of bickering over the details of the final document. Some of this is unavoidable; however, there are measures you can take to minimize the chances of this happening.

§ 11.14 How to Ensure Success in the Secondary Negotiation

Once the deal is concluded, repeat the major elements of the transaction at the closing to make sure there have been no misunderstandings.

If there have been, straighten them out on the spot rather than giving the other side time to mull them over and reflect on areas in which there might be a difference of opinion or interpretation.

If the deal requires detailed drafting, follow the oral agreement with a letter of understanding or agreement in principle summarizing all major points in writing. Whenever possible, have all parties sign the letter pending formal execution of the more detailed documents.

When drafting, be absolutely true to the letter and spirit of the parties' agreement. There is nothing more potentially damaging than trying to slip a major point into the agreement that is inconsistent with what the parties have approved. The entire basis of trust between the parties will be destroyed.

When dealing with points germane to the agreement that have not been expressly addressed, such as audit rights, indemnity, and so on, you should draft language to benefit your client whenever possible while at the same time being fair and not creating points that can become major issues of dispute. It is always best to negotiate these points with opposing counsel before the terms are submitted to the clients. This allows points of disagreement in the secondary negotiation to be contained between the lawyers. It also ensures that the lawyers will present a united front to their clients on these relatively minor matters, thus guarding against a last-minute snag that could kill the deal.

PRACTICE TIP: In all your drafting and secondary negotiations, you should be guided by good judgment, discretion, and fair dealing. Also remember that most of the time the other lawyer does not want last-minute problems any more than you do. This is why you should contain your differences whenever possible and not give opposing counsel reason to have to reopen the negotiation at the client level.

---

§ 11.15 There Is Always a Right Way to Win and Lose

Always remember that your integrity and credibility as a lawyer are some of your most important assets. Reputations are never built overnight, but they can be destroyed in a single day. No matter how the bottom line is tallied in a single negotiation, you can rest assured that you will have numerous opportunities in the future to put your negotiation skills and talents to work. That is why it is vital that you be very clear on the right and wrong ways to win and lose.

§ 11.16 Be a Good Winner and Downplay Your Success

When you come out ahead, whether the negotiation involves a long-term business agreement or the settlement of bitter litigation, be a good winner. One way to establish ongoing good will is to sincerely compliment the other lawyer on how well she handled the negotiation, or to send a letter putting in a good word for the opposing client. On the other hand, rubbing the opposition's nose in what may be a less than satisfactory agreement is a guaranteed way to make enemies for yourself and your client and create trouble down the line. If you must gloat about your successes, do not do it at the opposition's expense; it will surely come back to haunt you.

§ 11.17 Do Not Overreach

This point is of special importance in business transactions. As will be discussed in Chapter 12, imposing an unduly onerous contract on the other side even when you have the leverage to do so is a hollow victory that can sow the seeds for trouble later on. It is in the best long-term interest of both you and your client to negotiate deals that work in practice and not just on paper.

Overreaching is less of a concern in litigation settlements because there are fewer long-term implications. However, from the standpoint of your own future, you should be gracious in victory. You will certainly appreciate the same type of treatment when you are handed the short end of the stick.

§ 11.18 Be a Good Loser When You Have to Lose

When you are on the losing end of the deal, you always have the option of simply saying no and moving to the next best alternative. If that is not feasible and you feel you must agree to the negotiated terms even if they are less than what you wanted, be professional about it. Tantrums and derogatory remarks will not reverse the damage, but they can contribute to future problems.

12

Deal Making: Guidelines for Successful Business Negotiation

Spearheading mergers, brokering acquisitions, and negotiating every kind of license, assignment, and contract clause imaginable falls to the specialist known as the business lawyer. Whether working in a corporate legal department or with a private firm, the lawyer with a transactional practice frequently must rely more on his ability to shape consensus and manage compromise than on traditional legal training and knowledge.

A close look at the timesheets of some of the most successful business practitioners reveals that many spend the bulk of their time negotiating rather than practicing law. One well-known lawyer who specializes in representing professional athletes summed up the relationship between law and negotiation in a business setting as follows: "We all know the terms, clauses, and percentages by heart; it is simply a matter of how much you can get the other side to give up short of blowing the deal."

§ 12.01 The Two Measures of Success in a Business Negotiation

Lawyers negotiating on behalf of business clients are measured by two important criteria: (1) the ability to strike a deal and (2) the quality of that deal. Success or failure in either regard is computed in dollars and cents. Businesspeople accountable to corporate superiors, directors, and stockholders can ill afford to tolerate lawyers who are unable to succeed consistently at striking profitable deals for their clients. This is precisely why the successful business lawyer's ability to negotiate is critical.

§ 12.02 Business Bargaining Is Different

Negotiating contracts, licenses, and acquisitions differs significantly from negotiation aimed at settling lawsuits or labor disputes in terms of approach, objectives, negotiating style, and application of leverage. Sharpening one's skills in the business arena requires an understanding and appreciation of these differences. For this reason, it is appropriate to focus on the important recurring patterns and characteristics common to most, if not all, business negotiations.

§ 12.03 Everyone Has Something to Gain

Business negotiators approach a negotiation with much greater optimism than do lawyers engaged in conflict resolution-based negotiations. This is because everyone has something to gain from a potential business deal. In a business environment, the alternative to agreement is rarely a jury trial or strike, but rather a lost opportunity. This is not to say that the ramifications of failing to reach an agreement are not sometimes serious and, in certain instances, potentially catastrophic. However, such is usually not the case. Consequently, the overall tone of most business negotiations is upbeat and cooperative as opposed to the less-cordial atmosphere of conflict resolution negotiation.

The type and degree of potential gain will vary with the needs and circumstances of the parties. It may involve realization of such tangible advantages as increased cash flow, diversified production, acquired expertise, purchase of a distribution network, or the right to use a trademark.

Less tangible and more indirect objectives may include attainment of prestige, improved community relations, or higher corporate visibility. Regardless of the type of gain sought, the prospect of mutual gain in business makes win-win negotiating preferable to other approaches. This is in marked contrast to litigation, in which the plaintiff's success is usually attained at the expense of the defendant. In litigation, the defendant is a winner only if the plaintiff does not succeed. Even if the defendant scores a complete victory, she has only preserved the status quo. It is not difficult to understand the defendant's overwhelming lack of enthusiasm for win-win negotiation when the defendant's position is viewed in this context.

§ 12.04 Why Win-Win Works in Business

Because everyone stands to gain in business bargaining, there is a much greater likelihood that the parties will be more committed to a negotiated solution. On the other hand, each stands to lose in terms of time and opportunity if no agreement results. The prospect of mutual rather than unilateral gain makes problem solving and compromise much more attractive. As a result, ultimatums and harsh words are more likely to induce an opponent to exit the negotiation rather than to capitulate.

> ***Practice Tip:*** Stressing an "I win, you lose" approach is less likely to succeed in the realm of business than it might in litigation settlement talks.

§ 12.05 The Importance of Personal Relationships in a Business Negotiation

Because so many business contracts require ongoing reciprocal performance, continuing good faith between the parties is essential.

This is certainly true in employment, distribution, sales, or supply contracts. Even in corporate takeovers or acquisitions, good will is necessary to accomplish a smooth transition and to ensure that trade secrets and other valuable information are effectively and accurately disclosed. This is why preserving personal relationships is almost always an important underlying consideration for the business negotiator.

§ 12.06 When to Adopt a Hard Line

The roles mutuality and good faith play in the long-term success of business agreements underscore the need to approach this type of negotiation in a cooperative manner, stressing personal rapport, common solutions, and equitable compromise whenever possible. This is not to imply that hardball tactics and the leverage of sanction should never be used.

Adopting a hard line when called for may be the only way to preserve your client's integrity and ensure against unnecessary concessions. There is a dangerous tendency to confuse fairness with appeasement and rapport while avoiding tough issues. As stated earlier, the controlling principle governing your negotiating approach, strategy, and tactics should be flexibility and what is best for the client over the long as well as near term. This means reading the circumstances and taking action calculated to serve those interests most effectively.

PRACTICE TIP: Based on the recurring characteristics of most business negotiations, you likely will find yourself being more successful by stressing the positive and avoiding the negative. However, you should be prepared to be tough when the circumstances dictate.

---

§ 12.07 How to Plan for a Business Negotiation

Planning for a business negotiation can be decidedly more difficult and time-consuming than planning for other types of negotiations. The number and type of bargaining issues tend to be more wide-ranging, encompassing a much greater spectrum of possible objectives and facts. All of these issues must be identified, factored, and injected into the substantive talks. Candid and thorough conferences with your client will help identify the client's objectives, limitations, and time constraints. From this you should be able to set up preliminary deal points, secondary points, and trade points. This should also allow you to make an initial assessment of actual and potential leverage and construct a strategic approach for the opening move that is supported by tactical maneuvers. Finally, you should force your client to develop a walk-away position should the negotiations fail to achieve deal points.

§ 12.08 Selling a Fallback Strategy to Your Client

Forcing the client to develop a walk-away position can be difficult, in particular with optimistic businesspeople who are convinced that "nothing can go wrong." This type of client is often more interested in counting money than planning for trouble. Making the client deal with problem areas and potential failure is often viewed by the client as "negativism" or "lack of aggressiveness" on the part of the lawyer. Nonetheless, experienced lawyers know better. While there is no proven way to bring a "get rich quick" client back down to earth, there are some time-tested approaches that can help you get the point across.

"I'm paid to worry." The success of this approach rests on how effective you are at pointing out to your client that he is paying a lot of money to let you do the worrying. You should stress your genuine concern for the client and his business. This approach should be concluded with the standard, generally effective disclaimer: "Well, if the deal turns out to be as profitable as you feel it will, we can all laugh about this meeting when I run into you at the bank. On the other hand, worrying now won't cost you anything extra, but it could save you a lot later."

The horror story. An alternate and somewhat more dramatic approach is the horror story. You simply relate two or three unfortunate stories of clients involved in "can't miss" deals who refused to develop contingency plans to guard against stalled negotiations. The rest should take care of itself. It always helps your credibility if one or more of these former business whiz kids is operating an elevator or parking cars near your office. Depending on how good a storyteller you are, this approach will usually get the job done.

§ 12.09 Sizing up the Opposition

This is usually the toughest part of planning for a business negotiation, primarily because of the range and complexity of personalities, objectives, issues, and decision makers involved in the business negotiation. To illustrate, assume that Dotcom Corporation, a major high technology firm, has expressed an interest in acquiring your client, a small research and development firm specializing in solar technology, complete with patents, trade secrets, and employment agreements with key personnel. Further assume that your client would be interested in the deal provided Dotcom Corporation is willing to pay top dollar and further provided there were no other factors that would mitigate against selling. Insight into the personalities, motives, and circumstances behind Dotcom Corporation's offer will strongly influence the ultimate decision as to whether to enter into negotiations to sell and, if so, under what terms.

§ 12.10 Determining Why the Other Side Wants the Deal

One of the first questions you should ask yourself is: "Why does the other side want the deal?" In our example, the reasons are potentially wide-ranging and significant. Perhaps Dotcom Corporation is engaged in an ongoing expansion program through acquisitions. Dotcom Corporation might be looking for an end-of-the-year acquisition to reduce its tax liability. Dotcom Corporation might be seeking to buy expertise in the form of trade secrets or patents (which could just as easily be licensed). Or, Dotcom Corporation could be seeking to purchase a specific invention or patent application that could provide it with the necessary link to make a major breakthrough resulting in significant profits.

Sifting through these possibilities is important. Scheduled expansion or year-end tax write-offs are one thing; purchasing expertise that could be licensed or acquiring an invention or patent to facilitate a major breakthrough is another matter. The answers to these questions can provide a source of leverage, help determine the objectives of the agreement and the amount to be paid, and may even determine whether negotiations should proceed at all.

§ 12.11 The Role of Personalities

Aside from motivations and objectives, the personalities of the negotiators involved in the transaction play a key role in the negotiation's ultimate success. Consequently, you will want to know who these people are and how they are likely to act and react. We advise conducting your own DISC analysis based on the Marston principles discussed in Chapter 3. Additionally, do as much research as possible for clues about intangible behavioral characteristics, historical decision-making patterns, and the like. You can never know too much about your counterparts, both lawyers and their clients.

§ 12.12 Nuts-and-Bolts Issues

Finally, substantive issues relating to price, financing terms, transfer of assets, preservation of good will, and so on must be addressed. These nuts-and-bolts issues form the heart of any agreement and should be dealt with comprehensively based on a detailed assessment of all relevant circumstances.

§ 12.13 Sources of Information to Give You a Planning Edge

A limited amount of information about the opposition can be gleaned during the prenegotiation phase. The rest will be revealed in the opening move and later stages. However, time should be allotted in your prenegotiation preparation to inquire into the opposition's motives, objectives, personalities, and circumstances. Often your client can supply specific information or educated guesses on these subjects.

Literature produced by your opponent such as annual reports, press releases, and speeches by company executives are all potential sources of information as to their motivation for seeking a deal with your client. *Dun and Bradstreet*, *Standard & Poor's* and *Moody's* all publish directories and maintain information services that can reveal much about a company's financial condition and holdings as well as the personalities and backgrounds of its executives. *The Wall Street Journal*, *Barron's*, *Forbes*, and *Fortune* are all sources for current business and financial news. Government announcements, congressional action, and pending legislation are additional sources of information. Increasingly, most if not all of these information sources can be accessed online.

Once the raw data is collected, you should scrutinize it for clues as to your opponent's motivations and objectives and how your opposition's personalities are likely to affect the way the bargaining is conducted.

§ 12.14 A Deal Is Seldom as Simple as It Seems

Anyone who has ever sold a tract of land to an unassuming, low-key buyer for a modest profit, only to read later in the week about the plans for a new expressway or the location of an unexpected oil discovery on the very same piece of property, can attest to the importance of sizing up the opposition.

PRACTICE TIP: A healthy sense of skepticism accompanied by persistence and the ability to look beyond the immediate aspects of any proposed deal will pay big dividends when it comes time to close.

---

§ 12.15 Making the Most of Your Opening Move

Of the five primary functions of the opening move, three should receive special attention in business negotiation. They are:

1. Information gathering,
2. Identifying negotiation parameters, and
3. Initial use of leverage.

§ 12.16 Information Gathering

It is impossible to construct a final negotiation plan without sufficient information about the opposition. Sizing up the opposition prior to the opening move is certainly part of this process. However, in the great majority of all negotiations, only direct interchange between the parties can reveal the complete picture. If the opposition is experienced in negotiation theory and technique, you may never know the full story until the negotiation has been concluded, if then.

§ 12.17 The Eleven Questions to Ask in a Business Negotiation

To ascertain the information you will need, make sure you get answers to the following questions.

1. Who has final negotiating authority?
2. What is the extent of that authority?
3. Are there any crucial points of procedure relative to your specific opponent or your opponent's industry of which you should be aware and understand?
4. Is there certain terminology or are there industry standards and practices of which you should be aware and understand?
5. Is the opposition sincerely interested in negotiating an agreement or is it using the process for other purposes such as information gathering?
6. What are the opposition's deal points and secondary points?
7. What will they likely use as trade points?
8. What are their motivations, needs, and the limits of their objectives?
9. What leverage does the other party possess?
10. What type of leverage will be most effective against the opposition?
11. What role will personalities play in the negotiation?

Answers or at least clues to the answers to these questions should furnish sufficient information to formulate a realistic approach to the negotiation. The problem lies in getting those answers. Techniques for doing so are discussed in Chapter 5, "Opening Moves."

§ 12.18 The Role Hidden Factors Play

Analyzing information will help identify the issues and ranges that comprise the parameters of the negotiation. A key point to remember when identifying the other party's primary and secondary objectives is that they are often just as likely to be based on purely personal or subjective considerations as on objective criteria. Ostensibly, all business agreements are concerned with objective criteria such as price, quality, or service. However, for every objective criterion there is often a hidden subjective counterpart that figures into the final decision.

§ 12.19 The Case of the Jittery Purchasing Agent

For instance, assume a mid-level purchasing agent for a large corporation has the opportunity to buy a piece of business equipment from two different manufacturers. One of these manufacturers is large and well-established, and the other is a solid yet relatively new company. The products are comparable, but the equipment from the large manufacturer is the more expensive of the two. Further assume that the purchasing agent is not totally secure in his position and is subject to criticism from his supervisor that can affect his career progress within the company.

The purchasing agent finally decides to buy the machine from the large manufacturer, citing the objective criteria that the manufacturer has a proven track record and a reputation for quality products and service. The underlying subjective element is the purchasing agent's insecurity; he opted for the more established and familiar company even though it cost more, knowing he could justify his decision to his superiors in the event something went wrong. The purchasing agent's job security played a role in the decision-making process.

§ 12.20 The Most Common Hidden Factors

This is simply one example of the role hidden or concealed subjective factors play. Power, prestige, ego, acceptance, job security, and personal prejudice enter into almost all negotiations to one extent or another. This is especially true in high-level business negotiations involving accomplished, yet egocentric, executives.

PRACTICE TIP: Seek to ascertain both objective and subjective considerations likely to affect the conduct of the bargaining. Though often not as apparent, hidden factors can play a decisive role in the ultimate outcome of a business negotiation.

---

§ 12.21 Defining Parameters: Drawing the Boundaries of the Negotiation

Once you've gathered and analyzed the information, it is important to define the general parameters of the negotiation. This includes the other party's deal points and secondary objectives, as well as the degree of give and take that will be tolerated. Unlike lawsuit settlement negotiations, which primarily involve money, business negotiations are likely to have many primary and secondary issues based on objective and subjective criteria. These points should be identified to the fullest extent possible before any concrete offer is made or accepted. This potential multiplicity of issues is another reason why the opening move is so critical.

§ 12.22 The Pursuers and the Pursued

Parties to a business negotiation can be placed in one of two categories: the pursuer and the pursued. The pursuer is the initiator. He must first create interest in a deal if there is to be a deal. Once interest is established, the bargaining actually begins. On the other hand, the pursued need only react to the overtures of the pursuer. If the pursuer fails to generate sufficient interest, the negotiation is over before it ever really begins. This differs from conflict resolution in that the alternative to lack of interest in a negotiated settlement is a lawsuit or a strike. The more merit in the plaintiff's position, the more interest the defendant is likely to have in a negotiated settlement.

§ 12.23 Ground Rules for Representing the Pursuer

There are some basic ground rules to remember when representing a pursuer.

1. *Create interest.* This is your first objective. To be successful you must demonstrate how the deal will help the other party. This generally means that the leverage of opportunity will be most beneficial. Avoid sanction and uncertainty at this stage.
2. *Keep it simple.* Getting bogged down in complex details at the outset is a sure way to kill any interest in a deal. Stress the major points of your proposition in straightforward, easy-to-understand language. Provide enough specifics to give the other side something to react to, but do not paint yourself into a corner by getting too specific on substantive points.
3. *Open high.* Once interest has been established, always open on the high end of the spectrum. An experienced negotiator will expect this, provided you are not being totally unreasonable. Use of this tactic creates the trade points you will need to conduct an effective give-to-get negotiation.

A common mistake of inexperienced recent law school graduates is to formulate a "fair" initial offer with no downward flexibility. This leaves you no room to retreat and depends totally on the good faith of the other party to accept your initial proposal. In all but the most exceptional situations, this is simply naive and ill-advised.

An experienced business negotiator will be friendly, reassuring, and courteous while informing you that her client just cannot consider such an offer but would certainly be interested in a deal on substantially more advantageous terms. At this point, the lawyer who made the "fair" offer will swallow hard and turn slightly green, realizing he must either withdraw altogether or begin to bargain trade points that he never intended to give up to ensure reciprocal concessions.

§ 12.24 Ground Rules for Representing the Pursued

The lawyer for the pursued business client always has the initial advantage. This advantage can be parlayed into a favorable conclusion provided the lawyer seizes this initial advantage.

1. *Let the pursuer do the talking.* The more someone says, the more he is likely to reveal. The less you say, the less you are likely to reveal. By encouraging the pursuer to elaborate and be more specific, you are more likely to gain valuable information. This knowledge can later be converted into powerful leverage.
2. *Play it cool.* Never reveal your level of interest and enthusiasm. If you are very interested and show it, you can count on this fact being reflected in the price your client will ultimately pay. If you have no interest and show it, you are likely to alienate or discourage the other side into abandoning the deal. The best approach is to be attentive, courteous, and noncommittal.
3. *Control the timing and manner of your response.* Blurting out your reactions in a meeting or over the phone will generally have more negative implications than positive ones. Patience and discipline will buy you the luxury of time to assess and analyze a proposal at your own pace. You are probably best advised to punctuate your response with some form of the leverage of uncertainty unless you are prepared to close the deal. Remember that the other side is scrutinizing your reaction in search of certainty and security. There is no reason to accommodate your opponent unless, of course, it improves your position. If such is the case, do it.
4. *Open low.* The danger of creating an unreasonable floor is every bit as dangerous to the pursued client as the trap of an unreasonable ceiling is to the pursuer. Building in flexibility and creating trade points for the future is essential to the ultimate success of the negotiation.

§ 12.25 Leverage Techniques to Help You Take Care of Business

All negotiations seek to change the status quo. In business this means creating an agreement or business relationship that did not exist previously. The prime mover in altering the status quo is leverage. Of the four levers, sanction is probably the least effective, with opportunity being the most effective. The following represents several examples of proven leverage techniques geared to business negotiation.

Capitalizing on time investment: This is a commonly used technique related to the leverage of timing and uncertainty. It is particularly effective in helping to forge an agreement with an opponent who has numerous alternatives and is not particularly committed to reaching an agreement with your client. The key is to get the opponent to expend a substantial amount of time in the bargaining process.

In the event your opponent begins leaning to an alternative offer, point out all of the time she has invested in the negotiation that would be nullified. This technique tends to make your offer a more attractive alternative to starting over on another deal, which might or might not prove to be more advantageous than an agreement with your client.

PRACTICE TIP: In borderline situations, capitalizing on time investment can spell the difference between closing a deal and just coming close.

The vanishing opportunity: This tactic combines the leverage of timing and opportunity. It involves offering a tangible incentive or opportunity in exchange for a quid pro quo. The trick is to link the offered opportunity to a specified deadline. This imposes time pressure requiring the opposition to act or suffer the consequences of the lost opportunity.

Variations of the vanishing opportunity involve a tiered or structured withdrawal of the opportunity. For example, consider a seller's offer to finance an equipment purchase. Assuming the going rate is

8 percent, the seller's lawyer offers the buyer financing at 7 percent if the deal is concluded within one week, 7.5 percent in two weeks, and 8 percent thereafter. This technique often helps spur an indecisive negotiator to action.

The external deadline: This approach involves creating or adopting a deadline for closing an agreement over which neither negotiator has any apparent control. For example, citing tax consequences, you could set the end of the fiscal year as a deadline for concluding an agreement. Whether the external deadline is really relevant to the transaction or is actually beyond the control of the parties, once you can convince the opposing party to accept it, half the battle is won. At this point, the opposition will be required to take action. As the deadline nears and the opportunity to pursue alternatives fades, your proposal becomes increasingly appealing.

The masked sanction: For reasons discussed earlier, use of the leverage of sanction in the form of ultimatums or threats tends to be damaging to long-term relationships requiring good faith and mutuality. On the other hand, superior leverage of sanction is often effective in realizing short-run objectives. The "masked sanction" is designed to maximize short-term benefits without sacrificing long-term good will and rapport. As the latter half of the name implies, you deliver your demand and disclose the consequences to be suffered if the demand is not met. The only difference is that you tie the sanction to some force or circumstance beyond the control of your client. "If you do not accept our offer immediately, the bank will raise interest rates . . . the union will strike . . . the investors will withdraw . . . the stockholders will force our hand." In every instance, there is a sanction that will come from some independent source beyond your control.

PRACTICE TIP: Key phrases that can tip you to the masked sanction include: "It is out of our hands," "We don't like it either," "There is simply nothing we can do," "We'd like to, but. . . . "

The snag: The snag is a technique for injecting uncertainty into the negotiation. Often prefaced with an "Everything looks fine, but . . . ", the snag is often used to sidetrack a negotiation that is not proceeding according to plan. By focusing on a particular problem or a new bargaining component, the parties are forced to shift emphasis from the previous negotiating agenda to a revised agenda that you set. This technique helps buy time. It also helps take the emphasis away from troubling issues.

The straw man: This is a technique of raising or injecting into the negotiation seemingly important, substantive issues that are in reality only trade points that can be used to extract concessions at a later point in the bargaining.

The crisis: This is an application of uncertainty that seemingly puts the entire negotiation in jeopardy. It is often used in conjunction with communicating the walk-away position as a possible alternative to negotiated agreement. The crisis is a test of the other party's commitment to a negotiated conclusion. When used successfully, it tends to accelerate a final agreement.

Square pegs in square holes: This technique involves a mutual application of the leverage of opportunity. For example, assume the buyer and seller are negotiating the sale of a parcel of land. The buyer's primary concern relates to financing, with price being a secondary concern. Conversely, the seller is primarily interested in getting the best price possible and would be willing to finance the transaction. By making the effort to identify each other's mutual concerns, the two parties reach an agreement through joint problem solving.

The key to this technique is to find as many issues as possible that the parties can agree to or concede without substantially weakening their own positions. This is nothing more than the leverage of opportunity being used to achieve win-win results. Unfortunately, it is not always that easy to find common ground; when it is, the negotiators should make the most of it.

New ways to solve old problems: This tactic relies on creativity and innovation to develop new solutions to old

> problems. Assume you develop a sudden craving for a slice of lemon meringue pie. Because of an allergy, you cannot eat the crust, but prompted by your love of pie you long ago have made peace with that dietary restriction. In addition, because of strong feelings against wasting food, you are somewhat troubled to eat just the filling while throwing away the crust. As a result, when you make pies, you leave off the crust.

Because it is late, you rush over to the local bakery just before closing time. There is one last piece of lemon meringue pie in the bakery that contains crust. Next to it is a piece of paper that reads "sold." The baker tells you that he is taking the last piece to his grandson when he closes the bakery. At this point, it would seem that there is an impasse that would preclude the transaction. Just as you are about to leave the bakery empty-handed, the proprietor devises a novel idea to facilitate the transaction. Instead of cutting the pie in the traditional style, he proposes that the pie be cut in such a manner as to separate the pie filling from the crust. The proprietor assures you that his grandson only eats the pie for the crust since that is his favorite part. As a result you have his piece of pie without crust and without waste. The baker has his sale. Both are happy.

The baker charges you full price plus a quarter extra for custom-slicing the pie. On account of the scarcity of pie and the fact that it is closing time and that there are no readily available alternatives, you have come to view the piece of crustless pie as the equivalent of finding a hundred-dollar bill on the street, and you happily agree. As you head back home, you smile to yourself while repeating the old aphorism, "Some people know the price of everything and the value of nothing."

§ 12.26 The Secondary Negotiation: What to Do After the Clients Say Yes

Another characteristic of business bargaining is the secondary negotiation. After the major points of a deal have been reached, there remains the task of drafting the final documents to be signed by the parties. At this point, the negotiation tends to focus on contractual language—everything from audit clauses and notice provisions to indemnification language. Clients tend to view these substantive and procedural details as trivial, and lawyers tend to view them as crucial. More than one deal has been blown because of a failure to come to terms in the secondary negotiation phase.

PRACTICE TIP: The best technique for controlling the secondary negotiation is to assume responsibility for drafting the documents. This allows you to insert clauses and use specific language most favorable to your client. While you can count on the other lawyer to object to some of your clauses and language, he will likely accept much of it. In any event, the burden to react and object has been shifted to the opposition.

The key to making this technique work is to be faithful to all major and minor points on which there has been expressed agreement. If the other lawyer suspects you of changing terms to which you have already agreed, your draft will come under detailed scrutiny and you could be putting the entire deal in jeopardy. Once you have prepared the initial draft or proposed first draft, you should expect varying degrees of haggling over specific language. If you have established a good rapport, inspired trust, and conducted the negotiation with a minimal amount of personal animosity, you will likely find that your opponent will be less exacting on relatively minor points. On the other hand, a thorough lawyer will not approve anything that will prove detrimental to her client. Some lawyers are simply more thorough than others. Act accordingly.

§ 12.27 How to Handle the Closing

Because of the long-term implications of business negotiation, it is important that the negotiation be concluded on an upbeat note. Even if you have the leverage to push the other party into a one-sided agreement, if the agreement depends on future good faith and reciprocity in performance, consider your alternatives carefully. One must have an incentive to make a deal work. That incentive can be economic or personal, or both.

For instance, assume parties X and Y enter into a contract whereby both stand to gain. However, during the negotiation of that agreement, X's lawyer was abusive and rude to both Y and his lawyer. The personal bitterness engendered by the lawyer will, at least to some degree, carry over to the performance of the contract. Y will be much quicker to find fault with X's performance or be much more likely to retaliate at some later date. This is unfortunate, but avoidable.

In light of the importance of maintaining personal relationships, the following points relative to closing a business agreement should be kept in mind.

§ 12.28 Seven Keys to a Successful Business Closing

1. Do not overreach, even if you have the leverage and skills to do so.
2. Never make the opposing lawyer look bad in his client's eyes.
3. Allow the opposition to make concessions gracefully.
4. Downplay your successes and emphasize the other parties' victories.
5. Provide the opposition the ability to save face by making apparent concessions that can be magnified.
6. Repair any personal damage done during the conclusion of the negotiation. A word of praise for the opposing lawyer's professionalism and integrity or ability to handle a difficult situation will go a long way to negate any problems created during the negotiation. The same is true with respect to the opposing client.
7. Stress the positive and mutually beneficial aspects of the deal.

§ 12.29 What to Do When Faced with a Losing Bottom Line

All of the foregoing points assume you and your client emerge from the negotiations with a good deal. If, on the other hand, you find yourself at a disadvantage shortly before closing, analyze the deal carefully and objectively with your client. If the negotiated agreement will not put you in a more advantageous position as reflected by the deal points you set during the preparation phase, you are best advised to invoke your walk-away position, or at least indicate that possibility so you might gain a few last-minute concessions. There is never any magic in making a deal for the sake of making a deal. If you do not stand to gain from the proposed transaction, say no.

13
Negotiating Lawsuit Settlements

To most people, the trial lawyer is a personification of the glamour and excitement of the legal profession. Because of the mass media, everyone just naturally assumes that all litigators are courtroom crusaders who tirelessly pursue justice at every turn with an irresistible combination of quick wits and silver tongues. It is the best of Clarence Darrow, Perry Mason, and *Boston Legal*'s Alan Shore all rolled into one. Lawyers practicing on the litigation side know a much different reality.

As any trial lawyer will attest, litigators spend the overwhelming part of their time interviewing clients, drafting pleadings, taking depositions, and researching legal issues. Most of their courtroom work involves arguing motions or making routine appearances at hearings. The relatively few cases that actually do go to trial are usually far from dramatic. In the final analysis, more than 95 percent of matters in litigation are settled through negotiation. To put it another way, the average trial lawyer uses negotiation skills about 19 times more often than trial skills to resolve disputes and conflicts.

§ 13.01 The First Step to Mastering Lawsuit Negotiation

As in business negotiation, there are special considerations, patterns, and rules regarding negotiation theory and practice that apply only to lawsuit settlements. An understanding and appreciation of this special body of knowledge is the first step to improving your skills in this specialized area of negotiation.

§ 13.02 Everyone Has Something to Gain in Business

Business negotiators are optimistic by nature. Everyone has something to gain from striking a deal. Theoretically, and often in practice, there need be no losers in a business negotiation. This is why the win-win approach is so often emphasized by negotiation theorists and one important reason we stress its use in the business arena. At worst, failure to reach agreement will usually result only in a lost opportunity and an unproductive expenditure of time.

§ 13.03 Everyone Is a Potential Loser in a Lawsuit

By contrast, in the usual litigation settlement agreement, everyone has something to lose. For the defendant, the measure of loss is obvious. He faces the dilemma of having to pay the plaintiff to withdraw his claim via settlement or risk the alternative of having to potentially pay more in the form of an adverse judgment. A victory for the defendant is preservation of the status quo, often at the expense of substantial counsel fees and court costs.

Less obvious, but just as real, is the risk borne by the plaintiff. Because many plaintiffs' cases are pursued on a contingent fee basis, the unsuccessful plaintiff in a best case scenario loses time spent in pursuit of a fruitless claim. At worst, plaintiffs can suddenly find themselves exposed to liability by virtue of a counterclaim filed by the defendant's lawyer. More than one seemingly invincible plaintiff's case has been transformed into a voluntarily nonsuit in the wink of an eye by a well-timed counterclaim.

Emotionally and psychologically, both plaintiff and defendant are losers. Every lawsuit exacts a toll in terms of anxiety, pressure, animosity, and stress. No one is immune. Even so-called detached professionals such as trial lawyers, insurance adjusters, and corporate officers, who profess that litigation is just part of business, find themselves falling victim to the mental strain exacted by litigation.

§ 13.04 Why Win-Win Loses Its Luster in Settlement Bargaining

Because everybody involved in a lawsuit has something to lose—except, ironically, the defense lawyer, who is usually paid by the hour—it is easy to understand why the win-win approach is not suited to litigation-oriented negotiation. However, this is not the only reason why the win-win approach is often unrealistic in resolving litigated disputes.

Generally, a positive approach is necessary to preserve and enhance important personal relationships and to ensure the long-term mutuality and reciprocity needed to make contracts work. In lawsuit negotiation, however, the reasons for using a positive, less combative approach are not present. In most instances, personal relationships are badly strained or permanently destroyed by the time lawyers become involved.

Additionally, there are few, if any, long-term considerations regarding reciprocity and mutuality. Once litigation becomes an option, there is little worth saving. At this point, the plaintiff is usually trying to salvage her position with a monetary recovery to compensate for what has already been lost. Because the courts are involved, defendants, unlike their business counterparts, do not have the luxury of waiting in the face of a lawsuit. They must do something or risk having a default judgment entered against them.

As a result, the tone, style, and approach used in a lawsuit negotiation can differ dramatically from other types of bargaining. In order to succeed, you must understand and appreciate what is required in terms of strategy, tactics, and personal style.

§ 13.05 Unnecessary Aggressive Tactics Can Spell Trouble

This is not to suggest that a hardball approach characterized by demands, threats, and the leverage of sanction is the only negotiating style that will work in settlement bargaining. Indeed, such a style can be a recipe for disaster. More than one plaintiff's lawyer has made a bad situation worse by employing unnecessary hardball tactics against a seemingly helpless defendant. Always keep in mind that a smart defense lawyer with little or no leverage can still make life miserable for the plaintiff and her lawyer if given reason. This can range from looking a little harder for a counterclaim, to working the opposition into the ground by means of prolonged discovery, to making maximum use of dilatory tactics that can extract a harsh cost in terms of the time the plaintiff must wait to get money.

PRACTICE TIP: Our advice is to ignore a doctrinaire approach and do what is most effective. The watchword is flexibility, combined with recognition of the factors that make lawsuit negotiation a far different exercise than other, more positive types of bargaining.

---

§ 13.06 Using the Leverage of Uncertainty and Time

Uncertainty and time are the keys to understanding lawsuit settlement negotiation. Generally, both plaintiffs and defendants will seek to substitute certainty for uncertainty. A plaintiff will often forego the uncertain possibility of recovering a $100,000 judgment for the certainty of a $45,000 settlement. In addition to sure money, the plaintiff has also avoided the uncertainty that a jury could return a verdict of zero. On the other side of the table, the defendant who pays the $45,000 settlement has reduced his or her potential loss by 55 percent and has bought the certainty and peace of mind that goes with the dismissal of a complaint with prejudice.

Besides certainty, the parties to a settlement recognize the relationship of time and money. Even if the plaintiff has a good chance of recovering a $100,000 judgment, he must weigh the time it will take to conduct discovery, trial, and a probable appeal by the defendant. Even where liability and damages could be proven, all of these factors can delay the actual receipt of the money by years. Consequently, plaintiffs are usually much more willing to trade money for time.

PRACTICE TIP: The effective negotiator who understands the importance of uncertainty and time is in a much stronger position to use these two levers to effect more favorable settlements for his clients.

---

§ 13.07 Preparing for a Lawsuit Settlement Negotiation

Despite the pressure and stress associated with lawsuit negotiation, this type of bargaining is generally much easier to prepare for than the usual business negotiation, mostly because of the relative simplicity of the issues involved. In most cases, the primary issue is money. For instance, in personal injury negotiations between a plaintiff's lawyer and the insurance company that has been subrogated to the claim, the primary issue relates to how much, if anything, the plaintiff's claim is worth. Consequently, the entire negotiation hinges on questions of liability, extent of injuries, and the plaintiff's ability to prove her case. The likelihood and amount of settlement will be determined by the strength of the plaintiff's case based on these few factors.

On the other hand, the normal business negotiation tends to be more complex. To illustrate, consider the common situation in which a company is negotiating to acquire a smaller competitor. A multiplicity of issues are involved. Besides the bottom-line purchase price, the parties must deal with the identification and valuation of assets, financing terms, the status and transfer of outstanding supply contracts, employment agreements, trademarks, and trade secrets. There are also issues relating to liability for previous and prospective debts and defaults as well as tax, securities, and antitrust implications of the transaction.

This is not to say that lawsuit negotiation will always be necessarily less complex than contract negotiation. High-stakes business litigation involving a deal gone sour can take weeks, months, and even years of negotiation to resolve. However, under most circumstances, lawsuit negotiation involves fewer and simpler issues.

§ 13.08 How You Can Benefit from the Predictability of Your Opponent

Just as the subject matter in lawsuit negotiation can often be simpler than in other types of bargaining, the plaintiff's ability to predict the other side's actions and responses can be maximized with a greater degree of accuracy. This is especially true in cases involving insurance carriers. Every insurance company has its own internal rules, procedures, and unconscious habits. The totality of these characteristics and patterns make up the company's operating profile.

Some companies tend to emphasize resolution of claims through settlement more than do other, hard-line companies that prefer taking their chances in court. Knowing the insurance company's attitude toward settlement can play a major role in your preparation for negotiation. For instance, when dealing with a hard-line company, why waste your time with elaborate settlement overtures that will more than likely fall on deaf ears? Filing your lawsuit and pressing your case will probably be the only thing that will persuade this type of company to negotiate.

§ 13.09 In-House Rules and Guidelines Are Keys to Predictability

Beyond a company's general reputation, there are certain in-house rules of thumb or formulas that are used to guide their adjusters and legal counsel in settling claims. For instance, in certain companies, a junior adjuster will have authorization to settle claims up to a certain amount, without receiving approval from a supervisor. Once that level has been reached, the supervisor becomes involved.

After a certain point, which is generally after the plaintiff has filed suit, local counsel will be brought in to handle the negotiation. Insurance company employees, as well as the company's retained counsel, are bound by the philosophy and internal procedure of the client's company. The more a plaintiff's lawyer knows about the workings of a given company, the more effective she can be in adopting the appropriate negotiation strategy.

§ 13.10 How to Read a Company's Operating Profile

Some companies never make settlement offers until suit is filed and discovery begins. When dealing with this type of company, your knowledge of its business practices will lead you to the obvious conclusion that pressing for an early settlement would be useless. As a result, you can use your time more effectively on other matters while waiting to push for a settlement after discovery, when it is likely to be accepted. This is just one example of how insight into a company or law firm's operating procedure can pay off.

> ***Practice Tip:*** Knowing and understanding the general and specific aspects of a company's operating profile is an important part of your preparation phase. Being privy to internal information will give you an edge when planning your negotiating strategy and tactics.

§ 13.11 The Best Way to Find Out Is to Ask

The best way to find out about a company or law firm's operating procedure if you have had no prior dealings with them is to ask other lawyers. Most plaintiffs' bars have developed an unofficial "book" on each major insurance company and insurance defense firm in their locality. As would be expected, the defense lawyers generally do a pretty thorough job of researching and cataloging the traits, patterns, and habits of the plaintiff's lawyers.

Regardless of which side you find yourself on, you should always make a point of tapping this source of information when dealing with a company or lawyer with which you are unfamiliar. This type of information can often play a deciding role in the outcome of a particular settlement negotiation.

§ 13.12 Keep Them Guessing: Do Not Fall Victim to Predictability

As with most aspects of negotiation, the dangers of predictability can cut two ways. Uncovering the internal procedures of the opposition is not enough. To be successful, it is essential that you not be predictable. This means avoiding unconscious patterns and habits. Always try to keep the opposition guessing as to what moves you will make or how you will react to a certain maneuver or tactic. Even the cleverest move loses its effectiveness if everybody knows it is coming. Keeping the opposition guessing is your best insurance against ineffectiveness.

§ 13.13 Understanding the Defendant's Natural Edge

In lawsuit negotiation, the defendant always starts with an edge. To some, this may sound strange, especially in situations in which both the law and facts appear to be on the side of the plaintiff. Nevertheless, it is true. The defendant's edge derives from the burden of changing the status quo, which is squarely on the plaintiff. This requires the plaintiff to initiate every aspect of a suit, whether filing a complaint or actually proving the case in court. Only when it appears the plaintiff will be successful will the defendant pursue settlement negotiations seriously. This natural edge greatly affects the way plaintiffs and defendants approach lawsuit negotiation.

§ 13.14 The Barrier Defense and How to Overcome It

In a lawsuit settlement negotiation, the goal of any plaintiff's lawyer is to convince the defendant that paying less to the plaintiff now will be better than paying more at a later date. To do this, the plaintiff must constantly press the lawsuit forward to exert maximum pressure on the defendant. The defense lawyer, seeking to maintain the status quo, counters by erecting as many barriers between the plaintiff's and defendant's bank account as possible. When the plaintiff hurdles one obstacle, the defendant merely falls back to the next barrier, knowing all the while that time is running out and that the plaintiff's energy and resources are being tested.

Experienced defense lawyers know that anyone can file a lawsuit but few have the energy, commitment, or ability to push the case to a final litigated conclusion. The road from demand letter to an executed judgment is exceedingly long and perilous. A plaintiff has ample opportunity to stumble. Defense motions, counterclaims, depositions, and interrogatories can all be used for the dual purpose of exposing the weaknesses in the plaintiff's case and consuming time to preserve the status quo. In many instances, the plaintiff may withdraw or abandon the case for any number of reasons. Even if the plaintiff is successful at one stage, there will always be another barrier to overcome. The following chart illustrates the barrier theory of defense in a typical personal injury case.

Plaintiff's Action Defendant's Likely Response

1. Demand letter **1.** Ignore/deny liability/make accusations
2. File complaint **2.** File answer: general denial/counterclaim
3. Deposition **3.** Take additional depositions of plaintiff
4. Interrogatories **4.** Counter with interrogatories to plaintiff
5. Motions **5.** Countermotions
6. Jury trial **6.** Neutralize plaintiff's case
7. Jury verdict **7.** Appeal

§ 13.15 Patience and Preparation: The Two Keys to Hurdling the Barrier Defense

Experienced defense lawyers know that time is one of their best friends. It erodes the enthusiasm and resolve of most plaintiffs and many lawyers. Consequently, they are in no hurry to negotiate. Defense lawyers will only enter into serious negotiations once they are convinced that the plaintiff intends to go the distance and that the plaintiff's case is strong enough that the outcome is uncertain if the plaintiffs do pursue the claim to trial.

§ 13.16 Patience Is a Must

The patience of a plaintiff's lawyer and his client is absolutely essential to the success of any lawsuit negotiation strategy. This is difficult for plaintiff's lawyers, especially when they are acting pursuant to a contingency fee arrangement. But it is harder still for the client who has had little or no experience with the judicial process. The seemingly endless delay of litigation has disillusioned more than a few plaintiffs who had a meritorious claim. If you represent the plaintiff, you should take steps as early as the initial conference to lower the client's expectations and engender a sense of patience.

PRACTICE TIP: One way to help your client be patient is to explain to the client how the process works and what she can expect from the opposition. A realistic appraisal of the time considerations involved will help both you and your client determine the commitment each has toward pursuing the case. It is much less painful to decide early that you are not prepared in terms of time or resources to see the case to a conclusion. Making this decision can save months of money and effort.

---

§ 13.17 How to Use Preparation to Offset the Defendant's Advantage

Preparation is the other key to forcing the defendant into a settlement frame of mind. The plaintiff's preparation starts with a thorough investigation of the strength and value of the case. For instance, if the case is strong in terms of liability but weak in terms of damages, it makes no sense to mount a major effort to obtain only a nominal settlement. Substantial proof problems or circumstances that would indicate a successful counterclaim are other factors that could color the advisability of pursuing the claim in the first place. Lawyers who squander hundreds of hours a year on marginal cases that yield only token settlements can only blame themselves for their lack of bottom-line success. Plaintiffs' lawyers would do well to remember that they earn their fee when they close files, not when they open them.

Once the decision to accept the case has been made, it is vitally important to build the strongest case possible. Experienced defense lawyers are not easily intimidated. Too many young lawyers waste valuable time making threats and drafting half-baked complaints based on cursory investigation and haphazard preparation. Their time would be much better spent documenting the evidence needed to establish and prove each element of their lawsuit. As stated previously, only when a defense lawyer is convinced of your credibility, commitment, and the merits of your case will she move toward serious negotiation.

§ 13.18 Placing a Realistic Value on Your Client's Claim

Assuming there is probable or at least arguable liability, the true task for the plaintiff's lawyer in settlement negotiation is to place a realistic value on the client's claim. You can rest assured that the defendant is doing the same. Determining the value of a claim is especially important in cases involving insurance.

Insurance companies are in the business of resolving claims. Some companies favor delay and ultimate litigation, while others favor settlements. However, when faced with a situation in which liability is clear or highly probable, almost every company will want to settle. Indeed, insurance carriers have been held liable to their policyholders for acting in bad faith in not settling meritorious claims. When liability is clear or highly probable, the question is not whether to settle but only how much to settle for.

Numerous factors go into placing a dollars-and-cents value on a claim. The factors are essentially the same for both parties. While the following list is not exhaustive, it does provide a checklist of factors that you will want to consider when evaluating a case. Add to this list any additional specific information, local guidelines, or customs that might apply.

§ 13.19 Fourteen Points to Consider When Valuing a Claim

1. Presence or absence of insurance.
2. Policy limits.
3. Defendant's other resources or assets.
4. Possibility of the defendant's receiving indemnity or contribution from others.
5. Verdict expectancy as to subject matter and locality.
6. Settlement patterns of plaintiff and defendant.
7. Time value of money to plaintiff and defendant.
8. Experience, reputation, and credibility of plaintiff and defense counsel.
9. Plaintiff's ability to prove liability.
10. Extent of plaintiff's special and general damages.
11. Plaintiff's ability to prove damages.
12. Presence or absence of external and internal deadlines or schedules.
13. Aggravating or mitigating factors; emotional factors.
14. Any other specific relevant factors or circumstances.

Both the plaintiff and the defendant will spend the bulk of their prelitigation investigation and much of the discovery process trying to find the answers to these specific questions. Neither party should make or accept any substantive settlement offer until this information is compiled and analyzed. Above all, during this inquiry, it is absolutely necessary that the parties be as objective and realistic as possible. To illustrate the dangers of being overly optimistic or haphazard in the investigation phase, consider the case of Mrs. Hurt and her son, Ime.

§ 13.20 The Hurts and Lawyer Greedy: What Not to Do

The Hurts were involved in an automobile accident with a car driven by Joe Sloshed. Prior to the accident, Sloshed, who had a reputation of being a heavy drinker, had a couple of beers at a bar. According to the Hurts and other witnesses, Sloshed ran a red light, lost control of his car, and slammed into the Hurts' automobile, which was parked in front of their house. Mrs. Hurt and her son suffered minor cuts and abrasions, but miraculously escaped injury.

Neither was treated by a doctor. The police determined that Sloshed was not intoxicated at the time of the accident. The Hurts' attorney, Lawyer Greedy, ascertained that Mutual of Everywhere Insurance Company covered Sloshed under a $200,000 liability policy. Greedy, who is a teetotaler, has a very strong personal prejudice against drivers who drink. After hearing the Hurts story, he expressed outrage at what had happened and assured them he would teach Sloshed and his insurance company a lesson. Based on the foregoing information, Greedy filed a $750,000 lawsuit on behalf of the Hurts.

After a thorough investigation that included extensive discovery, the insurance company admitted liability and offered $3,000 to settle the case. The Hurts were insulted, feeling they were due a large settlement based on the circumstances surrounding the case and assurances their lawyer had given them. Greedy promptly turned the offer down, feeling that the prospect of a lawsuit together with the admissions of liability and aggravating circumstances would result in a substantial settlement offer. The big offer never materialized. The case went to trial on the issue of damages only.

Since liability had been admitted, the judge excluded all evidence relating to the circumstances surrounding the accident, ruling that it was irrelevant. The jury returned a verdict of $700 for Mrs. Hurt and $250 for Ime. Greedy, who was working on a 40 percent contingency, received $380 for 16 months' work. The Hurts went away full of resentment against the legal system, the defendant in general, and Lawyer Greedy in particular. Unfortunately, all of this could have been avoided had Greedy done his homework, maintained his perspective, and not made wild, unsubstantiated promises to his clients.

§ 13.21 Sources of Information for Assessing Your Case—and Your Opponent's

Assuming you have resolved to be as objective and realistic as possible, the next step to putting a value on your claim involves gathering the information you will need to assess the strength of your case and your opponent's defense. The logical starting place is with your client. You must make every effort to be thorough and professionally skeptical while at the same time showing compassion and support for your client. This can be a difficult balancing act. After you have interviewed your client, reduce his account of the facts to writing and submit it to the client for his approval. This procedure requires the client to consider and approve each detail he has given you.

Practice Tip: This is an effective technique for weeding out exaggeration and getting to the truth before making accusations and demands. After interviewing your client, confirm his story with other witnesses. You must first convince yourself that the claim has a reasonable chance of success; otherwise you may be on the road to nowhere.

Even the most thorough investigation will not give you all the information you need to fully assess issues of liability and damages. At this point, you must marshal all of your experience and resources to fill in the missing pieces. This is where an evaluation of the reputation, habits, and settlement patterns of the defendant, the experience and reputation of the opposing lawyer, and other such information will come into play. Discovery is another valuable weapon in uncovering specific facts and circumstances relating to the case. Finally, the opening moves of the negotiation itself will provide a great deal of valuable information.

§ 13.22 The Opening Move: Cat and Mouse Go Fishing

Experienced plaintiff's and defense lawyers often use the opening move to launch fishing expeditions for information in the classic tradition of a game of "cat and mouse." The following conversation is typical:

Plaintiff's Lawyer: "Well, Steve, I'd like to get together with you and resolve this accident claim we're handling which involves your insured."

Adjuster: "What about it?"

Lawyer: "You've seen the file. It's obvious your man ran the stop sign. It really just gets down to damages."

Adjuster: "From your version of the facts, it might be obvious. But our investigation indicates that liability is not as open and shut as you would have us believe."

Lawyer: "Well, let's put that aside for now. I'm primarily interested in what your company would be willing to dispose of this claim for."

Adjuster: "Well, I'm not sure we are going to make an offer. However, it would be helpful to know what your people are looking for. That would at least give me some idea of whether there is even any sense in pursuing this."

Lawyer: "You've got a copy of my complaint. We're asking the court to award $750,000."

Adjuster: "Sure, now what do you really want?"

Lawyer: "All I can get, you know that. However, I would imagine my client would be willing to take the policy limit less an amount to avoid having to try it."

Adjuster: And what would that be?"

Lawyer: "Well, I couldn't tell you until I confirmed the policy limit."

Adjuster: "That's confidential."

Lawyer: "You know I can find out in discovery."

Adjuster: "Well, I think the limit is $200,000, but I'd have to check. Assuming it was, how much would your client be looking for?"

Lawyer: "I'll tell you what, let me put the pen to paper and get back to you."

This type of conversation takes place thousands of times a day across the country. Here, both parties were sparring for little bits of information to help them assess how the other side viewed the strength of the claim. In this situation, both the plaintiff and the insurance carrier know that, in the usual case, the policy limits set an absolute ceiling amount on settlement expectancy. Consequently, they both know that in most cases the actual settlement amount will be substantially lower. In this particular situation, the adjuster wanted the lawyer to know that the actual policy limits were lower than the plaintiff thought them to be. Rather than just saying so, the two felt compelled to play cat and mouse.

> *PRACTICE TIP:* If possible, you should try to get the opposition to quote a settlement figure. This often gives direct information as to how seriously the other side considers the plaintiff's claim to be. The higher the figure, the more seriously the insurance company regards the claim.

§ 13.23 Substantiating Your Claim

Both plaintiff and defendant tread a fine line with regard to how much and what kind of information each is willing to reveal about the case. Generally, each side will try to establish the strength of her particular position while hoping to persuade the other side to reevaluate the case. The telephone is one method; correspondence is another. As mentioned earlier, a primary function of the demand letter is to substantiate the claim by providing your opponent with information that will lead to the conclusion that your client's claim is credible. A well-written demand or response letter can provide subtle information that will help you substantiate your position. You should refer to Chapter 8 on correspondence and apply the principles dealing with the uses of correspondence to substantiate your position.

§ 13.24 Finding the Settlement Range

Once the defendant has been persuaded to negotiate, and preliminary values have been assigned to the claim, the key to reaching agreement is finding a settlement range. This involves plaintiff and defendant reaching a broad consensus as to the value of the claim. If the plaintiff and defendant's general evaluations fall within the limits set by the other, a settlement range is defined, and an agreement becomes a probability. For instance, assume the plaintiff in a personal injury case is seeking damages of $100,000. He is willing to accept as little as $32,000, but feels the claim is realistically worth $45,000.

On the other hand, assume the defendant is convinced that the plaintiff has a strong case on liability with arguable damages. Defendant is willing to pay up to $35,000 to avoid trial and minimize expenses of defending the action, while feeling that the plaintiff might accept as little as $20,000 to settle the case. Consequently, a primary and secondary settlement range is established as in the following illustration.

The area of overlap between the defendant's high ($35,000) and the plaintiff's low ($32,000) creates the primary settlement range. This has the effect of narrowing the official stated differences between the parties from $100,000 and $0 to $35,000 and $32,000. The primary settlement range corresponds to a probable settlement of between $32,000 and $35,000.

Besides the primary settlement range, a secondary range of $45,000 to $20,000 is also established. Provided one or both of the parties redefine or adjust their high and low positions, the settlement could fall within this range. Depending on the amount of leverage and the effectiveness of the parties in using it, the various highs and lows of the parties will fluctuate accordingly. The end result will either be an agreement or the walk-away alternative of a trial. Of course, even if one of the parties walks away from the negotiation, the process of redefining the value of the claim can and often is renewed at some point prior to a jury verdict, and in some instances even subsequent to a judgment pending an appeal.

Failure to achieve a settlement range will usually result in a continuation of the litigation process until a range can be established or a verdict is rendered. To illustrate, assume the plaintiff's low figure was $35,000 and the defendant's high figure was $30,000.

Here, there is no overlap; rather, a $5,000 gap exists. Thus no settlement range is established. As a result, the litigation process would almost surely continue until either the plaintiff adjusted his low figure downward or the defendant raised his high figure.

In the usual case, as the trial date nears, uncertainty becomes more acute, and the threat of sanction more pronounced. As a result, the parties often find that matters previously thought to be nonnegotiable or firm suddenly become subject to compromise and reevaluation.

The lesson here, provided there is a genuine issue in reaching settlement, is for both parties to work diligently to establish a realistic primary settlement range.

§ 13.25 The Role of the Court as a Third Party

An additional factor when litigation is imminent is the court. Judges often act as catalysts in resolving the dispute. The judge's role can range from that of a mediator to a hard-sell third party.

In extreme instances, the high and low acceptable settlement figures are subject to reevaluation even as the trial proceeds. A poor performance by a witness, revelation of surprise facts, or an evaluation of how the jury perceives the testimony can prompt one of the parties to reevaluate its position.

PRACTICE TIP: Lawyers should remember that settlement is always an option up to and in some cases even after a verdict is returned.

---

§ 13.26 Basic Points to Remember When Formulating a Settlement Strategy

While there is no such thing as a foolproof blueprint for conducting a successful lawsuit negotiation, there are some basic points to remember.

Plaintiff's Strategy

1. Investigate the plaintiff's claim thoroughly.
2. Establish your credibility and substantiate your claim.
3. Demonstrate to the defendant your commitment to pursuing a verdict if a realistic settlement is not forthcoming.
4. Place a realistic value on your claim.
5. Open high, but be willing to readjust downward in a realistic manner.

6. Attempt to establish a settlement range with the defendant after making your opening demand.
7. Persist in your efforts to close the gap, but always be prepared to resume the litigation process if an acceptable settlement is not forthcoming within a reasonable time.

Defendant's Strategy

1. Make the plaintiff initiate action.
2. Use the barrier defense and agree to negotiate only if you believe the plaintiff will continue to press the claim and has a strong possibility of success.
3. Investigate the claim thoroughly.
4. Place a realistic value on the plaintiff's claim.
5. Open low, but be willing to adjust upward in a realistic manner.
6. Attempt to establish a settlement range with the plaintiff after making your opening response to the plaintiff's demand.
7. Persist in your efforts to reach a fair settlement, remembering that you have the advantage of the barrier defense.

§ 13.27 Three More Fundamentals for Successful Settlements

Beyond these considerations, both parties should observe the following points.

§ 13.28 Always Leave the Door Open

Even if you feel you enjoy a leverage advantage, never close the door to settlement negotiation. Things can change in a hurry. New facts, unexpected witnesses, an unfavorable jury are just a few of the innumerable things that can go against you.

§ 13.29 Talk in Ranges

The pitfalls of the floor/ceiling trap in business bargaining are equally applicable to lawsuit negotiation. Once the discussion gets around to concrete settlement offers, it is best to talk in terms of ranges rather than fixed sums. "We're looking for $30,000 to $35,000" gives you some maneuvering room. "We want $32,000" does not.

§ 13.30 Use the Client as a Hedge

When discussing settlement ranges, or offers, use the client to hedge. This is simply an application of limited authority. "I'm not sure the plaintiff will accept $32,000. I'll recommend it, but I can't make any promises." First of all, the ultimate settlement decision always rests with the client. Second, the approach gives you an out if the client will, in fact, not accept $32,000 or if there are other reasons to reevaluate the offer.

§ 13.31 Closing Considerations: Never Assume There Will Be a Settlement and Never Assume a Settlement Cannot Be Reached

No matter how close the parties are to a settlement, the litigation process continues until an agreement is reached, the parties sign the papers, and the judge signs the order of dismissal. Never assume there will be a settlement. Practical experience leads us to the conclusion that you should always be prepared to proceed with the suit up until the final order of dismissal. Often, lawyers banking on a settlement tend to abandon preparation for trial only to be faced with a collapse of talks. This results in losing points at trial or being forced to make costly and unnecessary concessions to salvage an agreement to dismiss.

Because uncertainty heightens as the trial date deadline draws closer, chances are that your best opportunity for settlement will come at the eleventh hour even though it appears that the parties are hopelessly deadlocked. This is why it is essential for you to maintain your level of preparation, keep your poise, and never assume that an agreement cannot be reached. By following this procedure, you will accomplish settlements you did not think possible. However, if the settlement fails to materialize, you will be ready to proceed to the walk-away alternative of a trial.

§ 13.32 There Will Always Be Another Lawsuit

If you are a trial lawyer, you can bank on the fact that there will always be another lawsuit involving a previous adversary. This means that, no matter what happens in the short run, there are long-term considerations to think about. As mentioned in previous chapters, our advice is to keep it professional no matter what the outcome. Your ability to conduct settlement negotiations with professionalism is essential to your long-range credibility and effectiveness.

Conclusion

As we stated at the outset, much of what has been presented in this book is neither new nor radically different from what successful people have been doing for years. Indeed, many of the principles and concepts dealt with in this book are based on common sense. These are precisely the reasons why the material is of value to you. In the final analysis, these principles work. It is your job to utilize them.

Our primary objective has been to apply these principles to the context of a law practice in the simplest, most direct manner possible to provide you with a comprehensive, ready-made strategy every time you participate in a negotiation. This book is not just to be read; it is a reference to be used. If you will take the time to understand and apply these principles, concepts, tactics, and ploys to the files on your desk, we are confident that your ability to achieve results for your clients will be enhanced in less time and with less effort. In a word, you will be a better lawyer. And that is what we are all trying to accomplish.

Index

A

B

C

D

E

F

G

I

K

L

M

N

O

P

Q

R

S

T

U

W

Y

About the Authors

X. M. FRASCOGNA, JR.

X. M. "Mike" Frascogna, Jr., is the senior partner in the law firm of Frascogna Courtney, PLLC that was established in 1972 in Jackson, Mississippi. He has been involved in international corporate litigation and commercial transactions, corpo-rate acquisitions and mergers, copyright and trademark matters, and practices extensively in the areas of entertainment and sports law. Frascogna is active in alternative dispute resolution, serving on the American Arbitration Association's panel of arbitrators and mediators. He has arbitrated and mediated numerous international and domestic commercial disputes. In addition, Frascogna has experience in hostage negotiation and is a frequent lecturer on the topic of negotiation.

He is admitted to practice before the U.S. Supreme Court, U.S. Court of Appeals, Fifth Circuit and U.S. District Court, Southern and Northern Districts of Mississippi, and all state courts of Mississippi. Frascogna served as a Bar Commissioner of the Mississippi State Bar Association from 1994 to 1997.

Mike Frascogna is a graduate of Mississippi State University (B.S. 1969, M.A. 1970) and Mississippi College (M.B.A. 1976, M.S.S. 1982) and the Mississippi College School of Law (J.D. with distinction 1972). He is a member of the American Bar Association (Forum Committee on Entertainment and Sports Law and the Section of Alternative Dispute Resolution) and the Mississippi State Bar Association.

Frascogna has been an adjunct Professor of Law since 1978 at the Mississippi College School of Law where he teaches an innovative course in negotiation to third-year students. He is the co-author (with Hetherington) of *This Business of Artist Management,* now in its **fourth** edition published by Billboard Books in New York City. The book, which is the standard reference work on artist management in the music business, received the coveted ASCAP Deems Taylor Book Award. *This Business of Internet Law* (with Hetherington and Shawnassey Howell) was published by Billboard Books in 2001. He is currently at work on his next book, *Entertainment Law for the General Practitioner,* (with Hetherington and Britt) to be published by ABA Books in 2010.

X. M. Frascogna, Jr., may be reached via e-mail at *mfras-cogna@frascourtlaw.com*

H. LEE HETHERINGTON

H. Lee Hetherington is a Professor of Law at Mississippi College School of Law in Jackson, where he teaches courses in torts, negotiation, trademarks and unfair competition, copyright law, and remedies. During his tenure at Mississippi College School of Law, he has been selected as one of the law school's outstanding law professors on five different occasions.

Professor Hetherington holds a B.A. degree from Millsaps College. He received his J.D. degree at the University of Mississippi School of Law and holds a Masters in Law with a specialty in trade regulation from New York University School of Law. He is admitted to the bar in Mississippi and New York.

Hetherington began his career in 1973 with Peermusic in New York City where he was Assistant to the Chief Executive Officer and House Legal Counsel. He also served as Acting Manager of the Nashville office of Peermusic in 1975. In 1976, he returned to his hometown of Jackson, Mississippi, where he became a partner in the law firm of Frascogna & Hetherington representing entertainment clients throughout the country. He also began his teaching career as a law professor at Mississippi College School of Law that same year. In 1984, he accepted a position as Vice President of Administration for Columbia Pictures Television Group in Burbank, California, where he was responsible for the day-to-day administration of Columbia's television operations. Hetherington returned to full-time law teaching in 1987. During his career, he has served as a visiting professor at Catholic University of America School of Law in Washington, D.C. He has also served as a summer visiting professor at Whittier Law School in Costa Mesa, California, and Southwestern University School of Law in Los Angeles, teaching respectively in their summer intellectual property and entertainment law institutes. While an executive with Columbia Pictures Television, Hetherington also served as an adjunct professor of law at Loyola Law School in Los Angeles. In addition to teaching and writing, he is a popular lecturer and seminar leader for corporations and law firms throughout the country through his company, Pathstar Education Group, LLC.

In addition to numerous scholarly and professional articles, Hetherington is the co-author (with Frascogna) of *This Business of Artist Management*, now in its **fourth** edition published by Billboard Books in New York City. The book, which is the standard reference work on artist management in the music business, received the coveted ASCAP Deems Taylor Book Award. *This Business of Internet Law* (with Frascogna and Shawnassey Howell) was published by Billboard Books in 2001. Hetherington is now at work on a new business book to be entitled, *The 5,000-Year-Old Formula: Negotiation from Moses to Next Monday Morning—The Rules Haven't Changed,* which will be published in 2010.

H. Lee Hetherington may be reached via e-mail at *hetherin@mc.edu*